Dear Reader,

As a thank you for your support, Action Takers Publishing would like to offer you a special reader bonus. Learn how to become an Amazon bestselling author by downloading "How to Become an Amazon Bestseller—Top Strategies Revealed."

You have a story to tell. It's time to tell it.

If you've ever thought about sharing your story and becoming an author, this ebook will give you tips for after you've published. This comprehensive ebook is designed to provide you with the tools and knowledge you need to bring your book to life and turn it into a successful venture.

Ready to become a bestselling author? Download your copy today at https://actiontakerspublishing.com/bestsellertips. As an Action Taker, you know there's no time like the present.

BS Tips

READER BONUS!

LeadHERship
UNVEILED
WOMEN LEADING WITH IMPACT

Email: lynda@actiontakerspublishing.com

Website: www.actiontakerspublishing.com

ISBN # (paperback) 978-1-956665-75-8

ISBN # (Kindle) 978-1-956665-76-5

Published by Action Takers Publishing™

Table of Contents

Nonprofit Beneficiary

Elimu Girls is a transformative nonprofit organization working in rural Kenya to empower young women through education, mentorship, and entrepreneurship. Founded in 2013, Elimu Girls focuses on breaking cycles of poverty, early marriage, and female genital mutilation by equipping girls with the skills and tools to lead independent lives.

At the heart of Elimu Girls is its two-year vocational sewing and boarding program, which provides students with national certification, life skills, and entrepreneurial training. Each graduate receives a sewing machine to launch her career, along with ongoing mentorship and a support network. This practical approach ensures that every participant leaves with the confidence, self-efficacy, and resources needed to succeed in her community—moving towards the goal of giving each of them a choice, a voice and a bank account.

Elimu Girls also addresses cultural barriers by fostering a safe, supportive environment where students can find their voice and power. Through mentorship, storytelling, and innovative activities like an annual fashion show, students gain confidence in their abilities and dreams.

Guided by the belief that "A sewing machine can change a girl's life," Elimu Girls offers pathways to financial freedom, equality, and lasting change. This mission is championed by a passionate volunteer leadership team and the vision of founder Cindy Rodriguez, an educator dedicated to empowering women. Together, they are transforming communities one girl at a time.

100% of the net sales from the LeadHERship Unveiled book will be donated to Elimu Girls. Learn more about Elimu Girls at https://elimugirls.com.

Introduction

Leadership is no longer confined to traditional frameworks or defined by rigid hierarchies. In today's world, leadership is being reimagined, redefined, and reinvigorated by women who bring their unique voices, perspectives, and life experiences to the table. *LeadHERship Unveiled: Women Leading with Impact* is a celebration of these trailblazers—women who exemplify grit, grace, and a steadfast commitment to transforming the way we lead.

This book is a collection of stories and exemplifies the power of resilience, determination, and authenticity. Within these pages, you'll meet extraordinary women who have risen through challenges, shattered glass ceilings, and embraced the nuances of leadership in their own distinctive ways. Each chapter is a journey, chronicling the triumphs, tribulations, and pivotal moments that shaped these leaders into who they are today.

You'll read about women who overcame deeply personal obstacles, from navigating systemic biases to enduring personal losses, and turned their experiences into growth and innovation. Their stories are a source of strength and inspiration, illustrating that true leadership isn't about being unshakable but about learning to rise stronger with every setback. These women don't just lead organizations; they lead movements, inspire communities, and empower others to dream bigger.

What makes *LeadHERship Unveiled* truly special is its embrace of leadership as a dynamic and human-centered journey. These women lead with their heads and hearts. They've harnessed the power of collaboration over competition, empathy over ego, and adaptability over rigidity. Their experiences reflect a new era of leadership—one that values diversity, inclusivity, and the unique strengths each individual brings to the table.

For readers, this book offers more than inspiration—it provides techniques for navigating your own leadership journey. Whether you're an aspiring leader seeking guidance, a seasoned professional looking for renewed energy, or someone standing at a crossroads in your personal or professional life, you'll find invaluable insights within these pages. Each story serves as a reminder that leadership isn't about fitting into a mold; it's about breaking it, crafting your own path, and daring to be different.

The women featured in this book are agents of change. They challenge the status quo, dismantle outdated paradigms, and create spaces where others can thrive. Their stories exemplify the transformative power of leadership rooted in authenticity, courage, and a vision for a better future.

As you read *LeadHERship Unveiled*, you'll find yourself inspired to take action, whether that's stepping into a leadership role, mentoring someone in your circle, or simply embracing your unique strengths with confidence. The lessons shared within these chapters will resonate deeply, urging you to view challenges as opportunities and to see leadership not as a title but as a mindset.

We invite you to embrace your power, own your voice, and lead with purpose. The women in this book have paved the way, and now it's your turn to step forward. *LeadHERship Unveiled* reminds us that leadership isn't just about making an impact—it's about leaving a legacy.

Cathy Derksen

CHAPTER 1

LeadHERship Unveiled: Grit and Grace in Leadership

Linda Fisk

As I crossed the finish line in front of hundreds of cheering volunteers and spectators, I glanced down at my watch and realized that I had achieved a personal best. I was filled with gratitude on that crisp, clear, sunny October morning, even though the marathon course included long sloping hills, and a couple of steep climbs, I was able to accomplish a lofty personal goal. I remember feeling a surge of pride that although I was now in my mid-forties, I was still able to sustain my body's endurance and vitality and push past any self-created limitations.

I had been running seriously for about 10 years, and training seriously for over two decades. I found that endurance sports, like marathons and triathlons, helped me forge a path that was not only defined by the finish line, but also by the profound personal growth and fulfillment that accompany the experience of pushing past any perceived personal boundaries or limitations. Whether you're aiming to conquer your first marathon, shatter a personal record, or simply revel in the joy of running, being an endurance athlete teaches you about the depth of grit and grace. And those lessons would be fundamental to the next 12 months of my life.

In essence, the mental game of marathons transcends the physical act of running. It is a profound exploration of the human spirit, a testament to the power of resilience, and an affirmation of the unwavering determination that propels runners toward the finish line. Running helped me overcome mental barriers, learn how to fortify my resolve, and embrace the transformative journey that unfolds with each stride. I didn't realize how important those experiences would become.

As many runners know, the hours and days after a marathon can be challenging. Often runners feel nauseous, achy, mentally foggy, or generally unwell. After this particular race, I remember feeling particularly sore, with acute muscle and bone pain, especially while walking. I decided to rest, hydrate, and go to bed particularly early, assuming that the pain was a normal and expected consequence of achieving a personal best time.

But, the next morning, I couldn't move my legs. I couldn't even swing them off the bed or create any movement in my legs at all. Initially, I was in shock and complete disbelief that my legs were completely unresponsive. After realizing that I couldn't move, stand, or walk, panic began to overwhelm me. I took a deep breath and called a friend to come over and carry me to the car for a quick trip to the hospital.

An MRI confirmed that I had suffered multiple complex injuries to the spine in my neck and back with an injury severity score of 64 out of a possible 75. My injuries included spinal fractures to the vertebrae in both my neck and back; ruptured, slipped, herniated and prolapsed discs; and fractured and splintering vertebrae creating bone fragments in the tissue surrounding the spine. The MRI showed bone breaks, with vertebrae that had come out of alignment and now tilted at an angle.

I suffered significant nerve injury due to parts of the vertebral body and discs pinching the spinal cord. The vertebrae in my back had slipped out of the spinal column and were placing pressure on my spinal cord. My injuries were extensive, and my prognosis initially seemed very poor due to being injured from the cervical to the thoracic and lumbar sections of my back. Essentially from my neck to my tailbone.

The spinal surgeon that was examining my MRI results said, "It looks like you were dropped out of a 30-story building. I've never seen such extensive damage. Were you in a car accident?"

"No," I replied in disbelief. "I ran a marathon yesterday. But my back has been painful for quite a while. I just thought it was a normal experience for someone of my age."

"Well, this is far from normal. I don't know how you were able to walk, let alone run."

In a burst fracture, both the front and the back of the vertebra are broken. Burst fractures are normally caused by landing on the feet after falling from a significant height, not from running a series of marathons and competing in triathlons. With this kind of injury, the spine is not able to support the weight of your body without causing the bones to shift or move and often causes nerve compression and nerve damage.

Injuries in sports often bring not just physical pain but also mental challenges that test the fortitude of athletes. The first step on the path of resilience involves embracing adversity with unwavering mental toughness. Olympians and elite athletes are renowned for their ability to channel setbacks into opportunities for growth. This mental resilience becomes a driving force that propels them forward, even in the face of seemingly insurmountable obstacles.

I am far from an Olympic or elite athlete, but the wisdom gleaned from the stories of other athletes that suffered a traumatic injury and staged a comeback served as a compass, guiding me through the exhilarating highs and daunting lows of the next 12 months. After three separate surgeries, two of which were more than 12 hours in duration, doctors inserted two rods and 28 screws to stabilize my spine, and fused three layers of my neck vertebrae.

Then it was time to embark on the exploration of what my recovery might entail. Although the spinal surgeon did not disclose his concerns about a full recovery prior to the surgery, once I began rehabilitation, he confided that, "You know, most people who suffered much more insignificant spinal injuries than yours never regain their mobility." At that point, I realized that the journey of regaining the ability to sit, stand, and walk extended far beyond the physical act. It would encompass a rich tapestry of experiences, emotions, and personal transformations — all requiring grit and grace.

The next 12 months of grueling rehabilitation highlighted the intricacies of the mental game I needed to conquer to regain my mobility. Everyday, I was exploring strategies to overcome mental barriers and cultivating a resilient mindset that helped propel me forward, step by step. And, while I celebrated each small milestone, I also experienced deep loss and grief knowing that my life had been permanently altered. Not only would marathons, triathlons, and scuba diving be beyond my reach now — I might not be able to walk without assistance.

In every area of growth, from your education to your career to athletic training, it's your level of mental toughness and determination that accurately predicts your level of achievement. Grit is a more reliable and accurate indicator of future success than any other determinant. Having grit becomes a driver of achievement and success — well beyond what skill and knowledge provide. If you are dedicated to achieving a clear long-term goal, and steadfast in your pursuit, undeterred by the sacrifices required, that is mental toughness and grit. And I was determined to sit, stand, and walk again.

Three months after surgery, I was at my surgeon's office for a routine check-up, when he said, "Well, do the best you can. But I wouldn't set high expectations. We have done as much for you as we can, but this is a steep hill to climb." And, while I knew he was trying to be consoling and supportive, I received that message as a challenge. I was going to be the exception to the rule, and fully recover my mobility.

We may have the talent, ability, and expertise to achieve greatness, but without determination, resilience, and perseverance, success will be elusive. By adopting a growth mindset, and developing the ability to persevere, you can see dramatic gains in achievement. Having the tenacity to pursue a long-term goal, knowing that you have the ability to improve over time, allows for the kind of stamina needed to persevere day after day, week after week, and month after month. The key is to recognize that your natural talents, physical ability, and giftedness are simply unmet potential, but with the application of persistent practice, you can achieve higher and higher levels of success. If you embrace the idea that setbacks, pitfalls, and adversity are part of the journey of growth, you can maintain your efforts, cultivating a sense of resiliency.

I knew my life would be different. And, while I grieved the loss of many aspects of my life that brought great joy, fulfillment, and reward, I also began exploring possibilities of what I might embrace in this new normal. I began using visualization as a potent tool in the arsenal of strategies to explore options, possibilities, and opportunities moving forward, harnessing the transformative power of the mind. I began using mental imagery to explore new possibilities like gardening, painting, swimming, and biking — and even walking around the block — envisioning my ability to surmount challenges with grace and resilience. By cultivating a vivid mental blueprint of success, I was able to approach rehabilitation with a sense of purpose and conviction, fortifying my resolve, and navigating the course with unwavering determination.

And, while I am convinced that incorporating the tenets of grit into my approach to rehabilitation that year was a fundamental key to success — it was equally important to embrace the concept of grace. In this definition of grace, I am referring to your ability to push toward your goal, while leaving room for failure. To really unpack this concept of grace, you first have to know, and accept, your own shortcomings, and failures. Indeed, failure is often why successful people achieve such remarkable heights of greatness: They learn from their setbacks, failures, and mistakes, and then get back up and apply these learnings to their next attempt.

You know your value because failure does not define you — in fact, failures are the very building blocks that make you stronger and even more valuable. Through grace, you can begin thinking positively of yourself, even though you will inevitably fall short of your expectations. When that occurs, forgive yourself. You can and will do better, if you allow yourself to.

After 12 months of rehab and another year of rigorous and disciplined exercise, I can sit, stand, and walk. Albeit I may walk a little awkwardly now. But this experience has underscored the pivotal role of mindset in shaping our narrative, and by embracing a blend of resilience, adaptability, and unwavering focus to surmount obstacles, I have integrated these lessons into my leadership style. I have embraced the ebb and flow of the journey, and I am grateful for the lessons that have impacted my perspective and shaped my approach to leadership.

My leadership style now reflects the experiences and the lessons of this journey, underscoring the art of embracing adaptability, leveraging setbacks as opportunities for growth, and recalibrating goals with a spirit of resilience that transcends the fleeting nature of obstacles. In fact, the significance of adaptability and resilience has emerged as a defining trait in my approach to leadership now. Unforeseen challenges, setbacks, and external variables often punctuate our journey, demanding a nimble approach to our ongoing recalibration.

Grit determines that life challenges will neither define us nor defeat us. It is the toughness, the courage, the bravery, the resiliency, and the spirit that drives us forward. It is the backbone, the inspiration, the steel nerve, and the vision that you cling to. Your grit is where your perseverance meets your passion. They collide to create your purpose, your mission, and your meaning.

Grace is freely given favor and mercy, a sense of generosity, and kindness, moral strength, a favor even when it is not deserved. It is understanding and forgiveness borne out of self-discovery and self-acceptance. It is an undeserved, unmerited, unearned embrace of acceptance. It always turns heads, opens minds, softens hearts, and leaves people in awe. And that is leadership unveiled.

In the five years since my multiple back surgeries, I have found a continued sense of inspiration and strength from the unstoppable women of LeadHERship Global, a confidential, and supportive community designed to accelerate the success of each woman in leadership.

LeadHERship Global enhances the leadership blueprint of resilient and tenacious women around the world and helps them embrace their power to be the best version of themselves — in work and life. I have had the opportunity to meet inspirational leaders, create lifelong friendships, and be surrounded by people that are invested in our collective success. And these women exemplify both grit and grace.

These inspiring connections with powerful women in business, politics, and entertainment provide priceless guidance about the pivotal steps that pushed them in the direction of their purpose, their mission, and their dreams. They provide practical tools, resources, and quick tips to show up, speak up and step up in your career and personal life, and step into your power.

Throughout my leadership journey, I have learned the importance of learning how to better serve others and genuinely support their advancement. I have become mindful of the opportunity and the responsibility all leaders have to serve their own advancement — by serving others. If you are a woman in leadership, ready to claim your power and change the world, then joining a supportive community like, LeadHERship Global, is essential. Join us!

Linda Fisk

Linda Fisk is a multi-award-winning CEO, TEDx speaker, 5x international best-selling author, WBAF Senator, TV and podcast host, keynote speaker, and university professor dedicated to amplifying and extending the success of other high-caliber business leaders. She is the Chairwoman of LeadHERship Global, a community of unstoppable women enhancing their leadership blueprint and embracing their power to be the best version of themselves- in work and life. At LeadHERship Global, Linda supports and guides ambitious, creative women to move in the direction of their purpose, their mission, and their dreams with powerful connections, critical support, practical tools, and valuable resources to show up, speak up, and step up in their careers and personal lives.

Connect with Linda at https://leadhershipglobal.com.

CHAPTER 2

Creating Impact While Reimagining Leadership

Cathy Derksen

I dedicate this chapter to all of the women around the world who are embracing the courage and tenacity to create a life they love.

"You never change things by fighting the existing reality. To change something, build a new model that makes the existing model obsolete."
~Buckminster Fuller

"What do you want to do when you grow up?" How many times did you hear that question when you were a teenager or young adult? We were trained to believe that choosing the path for the rest of our life was like choosing your favorite meal off the menu.

"Here are your options. Which one do you want?"

The options were presented to us as if there were only a few choices. We were led to believe that our decision would lock us in for the rest of our life. Wow! If we knew then what we know now that whole process would have been a lot different.

So far in life I have had three completely different careers. My original path took me to university and a 25-year career in Medical Genetics. I loved working in that field and the job I had was perfect for that time in my life. I had a schedule that worked well with my family's needs. I had great benefits and plenty of holiday time.

As the years went by, my situation changed. I found myself in an abusive marriage and a toxic work environment. The pressures of these negative factors led me to give serious reconsideration to my options at that time. Even after all of those years, I still felt like I had to pick a career option from the list in front of me and I saw myself as someone who would always work under someone else. I didn't see myself in a leadership role. I didn't see the infinite list of opportunities that I now know exist.

My vision for my future has changed and my definition of leadership has been expanded and deepened by the amazing women I've met during the past few years. Immersing myself in several women's organizations has opened my eyes to the changes women are creating in leadership. I've met so many women who are frustrated and disillusioned by the archaic models of leadership traditionally seen in so many organizations. I now see women transforming leadership at every level in business and community. Over time, we have been replacing those old models with a fresh new look and feel.

Women are taking on leadership from new perspectives with new strategies and styles. Collaboration and mentorship have replaced traditional competition and the 'survival of the fittest' mentality. As diversity, equity, and inclusion have become mainstream conversations, we have embraced a wide range of approaches to leadership. As I look back over my decades in the workforce, there are many examples of good leaders as well as ones who had a very destructive impact on their staff and clients. As I mentioned earlier, my original career was in healthcare. I specialized in clinical genetics and spent 25 years working in hospital labs and public education. My second career was in financial planning, working in large banks and investment companies. When I chose to leave those employers, my decision was greatly influenced by the negative impact of working under destructive leadership. I was dealing with physical and mental health issues associated with toxic work environments.

During those two chapters of my working life, I didn't see an option for bringing change to those workplaces, and I didn't feel I had any power or voice to impact the leadership model I worked under. The only option I could see for saving myself from the chronic health issues brought on due to the stress of working in those situations was to remove myself from the environment. My careers in healthcare and finance were both cut short as a direct result of leadership models that treated employees as little more than a cog in the wheel of a large organization.

In 2020, I made the massive decision to leave behind the life of being employed by those large companies. I chose to set out on my own to create a career that met my needs and brought joy to my life. My journey as an entrepreneur has had its share of ups and downs, but the lessons I've learned along the way have been life changing.

I've witnessed many women who have chosen to either step up into a role that allows them to make changes in their current workplace or have walked away from organizations to create a new business that exemplifies the values and behaviors they choose to live by. They are not just taking a seat at the leadership table to create change, they are starting a whole new table that allows them to set the ground rules.

In today's leadership models, the focus is on tapping into the strengths of each member of the organization and replacing competition with collaboration. These changes allow each member to feel valued and respected; these leadership styles encourage team members to feel connected and supported, consequentially leading to more productivity and less staff turnover.

Honoring diversity in the workplace has also become a critical factor in creating more success on many levels. A wide variety of perspectives, attitudes, and lived experiences allows a team to be more creative and incorporate new ideas into their decision-making process. Another significant trend in leadership styles that has been part of this evolution is the shift from looking at leadership as a top-down hierarchy. The old model, having one person at the top with all of the control, has shifted to a model that sees many team members having various levels of leadership opportunities in their jobs.

In bringing together the team of authors in this book, my goal is to spotlight and highlight a small group of women who are transforming leadership in business and community. Their stories demonstrate their journey and how they became inspired to take on leadership roles in their life at work and at home. My vision for this book is to inform and inspire women around the world to take on their own journey as leaders in every aspect of their lives.

As I've taken my own path as a leader, I have developed many new skills and learned lessons that will impact the rest of my life. I have left behind the work environments that have made me feel disrespected and taken advantage of, and I've developed my own business that allows me to create the community and atmosphere that supports me and my team to excel in our passions.

Here are a few of the lessons I've learned along the way:

Embrace Your Unique Style

We all have skills to develop as we become leaders, but the lessons we learn should be focused on developing and enhancing our own style. When I first stepped into leadership roles, I was told I needed to be big and flashy. Whenever I attempted to develop that style, it felt inauthentic and uncomfortable. I learned that being myself and sharing my passion as authentically as possible is key.

Think Outside of the Box

Most of my life, I believed my career path needed to be made up of pre-existing job descriptions. Now, I know that being creative in bringing your vision to life is so much more fun. The work I'm doing now, creating these multi-author book projects, was birthed from my passion for supporting women in sharing their stories and stepping into new possibilities. There were no guidelines to follow or job descriptions to stick with. My vision became my reality. Now, the work I'm doing impacts women around the world and shares voices that haven't been heard.

Build a community of Support and Encouragement

As you step into new areas of leadership, you will go through many challenges, and you'll need to navigate many obstacles along the way. It is critical to have a community around you that will provide a safe space to share your challenges, vent your frustrations, and remind you that you're not alone. Together, we can lift each other.

Be Open to Collaboration and Mentorship

Find ways that you and your community can work together and provide complimentary services. You can achieve a new level of success by bringing together each person's expertise.

Be Courageous and Bold

Creating change in the world always comes with making major decisions and taking action in ways that aren't familiar or comfortable. Step into these challenges with confidence. Feel the fear and do it anyway.

Dream Big

Allow yourself to create a big vision of the future you aim to create without the limiting beliefs that have kept you playing small.

Be a Role Model for Others

As you step into various levels of leadership in your life, other people will take notice. By stepping into a new version of yourself, you are giving other women the motivation and example to follow in your footsteps. Sharing your story and being open to supporting others creates a ripple effect of positive impacts on the world.

Self-leadership needs to be the foundation of all leadership possibilities. Learning how to manage yourself, your mindset, your emotional intelligence, and your social responses will establish your strength as a leader.

I'm excited and inspired by the changes I have seen in leadership as women take their places at all levels and lead with their hearts. The future is looking bright as we learn to collaborate and support each other in new opportunities and possibilities. I hope you will join the movement and take your place in leading and inspiring change in your workplace, community, and family.

Cathy Derksen

Cathy Derksen is the founder of her company, Inspired Tenacity Global Solutions Inc. She is a Disruptor and Catalyst dedicated to improving the lives of the women in her community and around the world. Cathy helps women rediscover their brilliance, find their voice, and step into new possibilities.

A decade ago, Cathy transformed her career from working in Medical Genetics for 25 years to financial planning so that she could focus on helping women create personal success. Over the years, Cathy has followed her passion for learning and has become certified in counselling, leadership, success principles, and strategies for overcoming limiting beliefs and mindset. Her programs at Inspired Tenacity allow her to blend all of her skills to amplify the impact of her work.

Cathy is now an international speaker and 17x #1 bestselling author. She has created a platform for women to share their wisdom and inspiring stories in collaborative books, taking them from chapter concept to bestselling author in a simple, exciting process.

Cathy has two children (28 and 29 years) and 2 fur-babies. She lives near Vancouver, Canada.

She enjoys spending time in nature, travelling, meeting new people, and connecting with her global community.

Connect with Cathy at www.inspiredtenacity.com.

CHAPTER 3

The Hero in My Own Story

Angela Fowler

To all those who expected the best from me,
blindness, or no blindness.

Sometimes, it's hard to be blind. I know what you're thinking, but that isn't the reason. It's hard to be blind because of the mixed messages often sent to you by society. You are told "you can do anything!" You are rewarded with effusive praise for accomplishing ordinary things and made excuses for if you fall short. At the same time, your ability to do basic things is doubted. You are often asked: "How do you do that if you can't see?" If you're good at something, you are heralded as amazing, but if you are bad at something it is attributed to blindness.

This contradiction colored much of my childhood and young adulthood, skewing my perspective of who I was, what I was and was not good at, and what I needed to do to succeed in business and in life.

But no more. As I have gotten older and wiser and grown into my role as a leader, I have learned to turn all that noise down. I am guided not by the confused messages of society but by some guiding principles I have developed through hard experience and deep thought, and from which I hope all good leaders take wisdom. For my strength as a leader has nothing to do with blindness, and everything to do with the human being I choose to be.

The Guiding Principles

Throughout much of my life I held in high regard what others thought. Though uninformed, their expectations shaped my own, and their endorsements were the fuel which drove me. Once I decided to take control of my own life and live according to the guiding principles I knew to be true, I was able to truly find success.

- Know yourself: know your strengths and weaknesses and don't waste time doing things you're not good at just to prove a point.

- Everyone falls on their face sometimes: get up, dust yourself off, and keep going.

- To quote the old westerns, "You have to earn your spurs." It takes time, patience, and diligence to build the credibility that will lead to clients investing in you.

- Lead with understanding: know that most people have good intentions, they often just lack information.

- Be tough when you need to be: if you know something isn't right, stand your ground.

- Be the hero in your own story: take responsibility for your own life. Remember, excellence trumps bias.

Know Yourself

I went through much of my early life with a chip on my shoulder. I wanted to prove to everyone that blind people could do everything sighted people could do. But as I grow older, I realize that everyone has strengths and weaknesses. I have come to know my gifts and my shortcomings. I know what I can do with little effort, what I can do with difficulty, and what I can't do barring a miracle.

This has made me a more efficient businesswoman. I have stopped pressuring myself to do the tasks I am not so good at just to prove a point. Instead, I focus on the tasks I am best at, such as giving presentations on accessibility and solving unique accessibility challenges. I have hired others, some of whom are also blind, to do the tasks I am not as good at or don't enjoy, such as email marketing, or posting consistently to social media. This frees me up to work in my zone of genius and give the best of myself to my business and to my clients.

Everyone Falls on Their Face Sometimes

They say that which doesn't kill us makes us stronger, and my failed venture of 2022 certainly made me stronger. Pure Access, as it was known, was a partnership between three co-founders, one of whom had a completely different view of what an accessibility company should be. We had fundamental disagreements about what services to offer and what our target audience should be. As the CEO, I tried to accommodate everyone. As a result, we tried to be all things to all people. We tried to sell numerous unrelated services to different audiences at the same time, and potential clients had difficulty understanding exactly who we were and what we did.

We were also overspending. This compelled us to rush into sales and marketing before building concrete offers, selling promises in which potential clients could not trust. Though our intentions were good, the planning simply wasn't there, and everyone saw it.

I suppose it comes as no surprise then that Pure Access collapsed under its own weight.

Disagreements between the partners became too much to overcome. There was more money going out than our personal budgets could handle. After some drama with which I will not bore you, the partnership broke apart.

Every New Year's Eve I post an end-of-year summary on social media. It always ends something like this: "Here's to the struggles that make us stronger, the changes that make us wiser, and continued striving for a better life." It was never truer than in 2022. The fall of Pure Access could have been the end of my dreams, but I took wisdom from it, gained strength from the struggle, and in 2024, came back for another round.

Start Small, Stay Sustainable

After licking my wounds for a while, I began to build the foundation for my next business. With hardly a word to anyone, I created a website, got a business license, and created my flagship course series, Access for Everyone. I also put plans in place for some in-person webinars and group coaching sessions. I wanted to bring tangible offerings to the market that potential customers could easily understand.

I also significantly cut some of the business expenses that had brought Pure Access to the brink. My motto was: "Start small, stay sustainable, make sure you have the luxury of time if that first client doesn't immediately come." It is truly liberating to be able to work deliberately, to not be pressured by circumstances into making an impulsive decision.

One thing about being told you're amazing all the time is that a part of you begins to take it for granted. It becomes hard to accept the reality that we all start out at the bottom. But it's okay to be the little guy. Fewer people depend on you for their livelihood, you have a smaller sphere of influence, and when you make mistakes, which you inevitably will, those mistakes are less impactful and more easily forgiven.

You Have to Earn Your Spurs

Often things come to blind children too easily. I remember as a child getting out of some school assignments just because I said they were hard. The teachers would assume it was hard because I was blind, when in fact it was probably just one of those annoying tasks that we all have to push through. This left me with the subconscious belief that things in life should be easy.

But people aren't going to invest in your business because of an emotion-based desire to see the blind girl succeed. They'll root for you, they may be generous with their time and advice, but in order to get them to sign on the bottom line you have to establish credibility. That is done through time, patience, and effort.

Not everyone has mixed up expectations when it comes to blindness. These days I have surrounded myself with coaches and mentors who will give me the pure unvarnished truth. If I want to approach a potential client with a half-baked offer, my business coach will lovingly say "you're not ready yet." Then we'll work out a plan to get there. The beautiful thing is, because I'm committed to starting small and staying sustainable, I can afford to work the process.

Lead With Understanding

I've written a lot about society's misunderstanding of blind people and the negative effect it has on us, but how did we get here? Most people don't have bad intentions, they just aren't properly informed. They don't know what blind people can do because they never had the opportunity to observe a blind person doing it.

I take that same wisdom into my work teaching businesses to make their products and services accessible. In 2021, I got a job as an accessibility specialist working with web designers and developers who had varying degrees of knowledge about accessibility. Once I showed them why it was important, they were all eager to learn. So, I assume good faith when talking to business leaders. I operate on the premise that most people want to do the right thing, they just don't know what the right thing is. Meeting them there, I can get them to truly invest in accessibility, not just do the minimum because of a legal mandate.

Be Tough When You Need to Be

While you seek to understand and then to inform, sometimes you have to look people in the eye and say, "this isn't happening." In the midst of my failed 2022 venture, there were those on my team who wanted to go into debt to get a discount on book publishing services. This was unsustainable. We were operating on a shoestring budget, and having just recovered from serious debt, I didn't want to go back. This was one area where I could not be accommodating. I drew a hard line and thank God I did. A few weeks later, the partnership broke up, and the business officially failed.

There is much written about consensus, about talking through an issue until everyone comes to an agreement. But I believe God gives us life experience so that we may gain wisdom and puts us in positions of trust so that we may use it. I didn't go through all those sleepless nights with too much debt and too little money for nothing. I knew what was right, and knew I needed to draw the line.

You Are the Hero of Your Own Story.

In 2020, I was working a job which wasn't paying the bills, and debt was piling up. Enough was enough. Though I got all my previous jobs with the help of government funded employment programs or with help from someone I knew in the organization, it was time to strike out on my own. I put myself out there, interviewed, and got a job which nearly doubled my income. I paid off debt, put some money in savings, and despite a rocky 2022, I am now financially secure enough to run my company without taking on debt or depending on government programs. Only when I decided to take control of my own life, to depend on neither my network nor the government to save me, was I able to shake off society's expectations and be the businesswoman I am today.

Excellence trumps bias. Whatever people believe about the capabilities of blind people, their minds are changed more by what I do and how I run my business than anything else. If I play to my own strengths, work hard to earn my spurs, get back up when I'm knocked down, lead with understanding yet stand on principles when necessary, that excellence will shine through any bias someone else may have.

Conclusion

These core principles have nothing to do with blindness. They are nuggets of wisdom that I gleaned only when I decided that blindness was not the lens through which I would look at my life. We all have things for which people might misjudge us. But excellence trumps bias. You have the power to choose what kind of person you will be. What principles will you live by? What experiences will give you the strength and the resilience to pick yourself up when life knocks you down so that you keep going? It's different for everybody. But take a look around your life. Find ways you can grow into your own leadership. Be the hero in your own story.

Angela Fowler

Angela Fowler is a popular coach, consultant and speaker who shows organizations how to increase their bottom line by leveraging the power of accessibility to tap into the $2.1 trillion buying power of people with disabilities. As a businesswoman who is also totally blind, she has a unique insight into what it takes for regular everyday businesses to tap into a market which they may not fully understand or readily think is available to them. With humor and straight talk tempered with patience, she shows organizations how to make the necessary adjustments, often with a lot less effort than they think.

Angela's courses offer common-sense, cost-effective solutions to help businesses make their products and services accessible to people with disabilities and more user-friendly for everyone. Her philosophy is that most people want to do the right thing, they just don't know what the right thing is.

Angela runs her coaching and consulting business from her home in Northern California, which she shares with her 18-year-old son, whose life seems to barely include her, her feisty kitten, who very clearly prefers her son, and her loving dog of indeterminate breed who thinks she's God's gift to doggie-kind and cannot get enough of her company. When she's not working, she enjoys true crime, sports, and cooking the best tri-tip on God's planet low and slow on the barbecue.

Connect with Angela at http://www.reallifeaccess.com.

CHAPTER 4

An Inside Job

Ari Wells

Dedicated to my son Jaden — Be Brave! Everything you
need is inside you already. Love Mommy

Growing up and navigating adulthood, I encountered so many life situations where I wished I had someone to physically direct me as to how to make the best decision. I was looking for a survival guide for life. Fast forward and now I realize I am God's daughter, a mother, a wife, an entrepreneur and business owner, or any other title that is required. So, I'm going to share with you some of the lessons I have learned.

You Teach People How to Treat You.

That statement is a mouthful, right? When I was getting married for the second time, my Aunt Jean told me, "Start out how you want to

31

hold out." When she said it, I thought I understood what she was say-ing, but I did not. From the time I was a little girl, I picked up this bad habit of doing for others what I wished would have been done for me. Slowly read that again to yourself and sit with the thought for a second. It sounds harmless, right? Unlearning that detrimental and sometimes toxic behavior was one of the most freeing moments for me as an adult.

So many times, we have these events that happen in our childhood that we say to our smaller selves "never again" and we work so hard to not become what, or who, hurt us that we don't learn the lesson of balance.

As a child, I experienced lots of loneliness and felt I had to do so many scary things by myself that I promised myself that when I got older no one I loved would have to feel that way. While it's a noble thought, it's not realistic. Anything done in excess, even if it's a good thing, can be bad for you. So, what did that look like for me as I grew older and became an adult? I became so loyal to others that many times I would betray myself and fall on the sword trying to be everyone else's hero but never my own.

In my mind, well that's what you should do if you love someone, you put them first. Sounds like a noble idea, right? To martyr yourself for the good of others? But consider this: is that what the other person truly needs or is it to make you feel better because you have a wound you haven't dealt with? Next question, and this one is huge: Did they ask you for your help? Many times, at the end of a situation or misunderstanding, I've done for someone else what I wished someone would have done for me. And guess what? That person did not care about what I cared about. I was way more invested than they were. You cannot truly help someone by acting based on what you wish someone had done for you, especially when you are still holding onto your own wounds.

I carried this behavior into my leadership or even into work sometimes and wondered why I felt burned out. Many times, this caused me to burn my candles at both ends, not realizing, or respecting my own limitations, by trying to show up for others or the job the way I wished people would have shown up for me. The truth is, that version of me was not the best version of me as I was betraying myself every time I poured from my cup knowing it was empty. I was not respecting myself, and I was teaching the people around me to never value me or consider the sacrifices I was making. How can you expect others to respect or consider you if you don't respect or consider yourself? How can you lead others when you are not effectively leading yourself?

I had to take an honest self-assessment and therapy. Being honest with myself and determining if I really had a healthy self-image was where I started. Did I really see my own value or was I looking for others to validate me by the performance I gave? What I learned was external validation is never going to fulfill you. You will always need more validation — like someone who experiences addiction and chases the very first high they experienced. Therapy is essential. Sorting out the root, or why you do the things you do, is imperative to growing, and unlearning toxic or self-sabotaging behaviors. I don't have everything figured out but what I do know is unlearning toxic behaviors and unlearning the distorted self-image we have of ourselves is the beginning of true freedom.

No Perfectionism. Aim for Excellence.

Perfectionism was and sometimes is still a thing I struggle with internally. Some of the perfectionism is learned from growing up and some comes from my occupation as a Registered Nurse. As a child I never really felt like I was pretty, but one thing I did know was that I was smart. Once again, there was this moment in my 5th grade social studies class when I was laughing with a group of kids, trying to fit in, and the teacher got frustrated with us. She stopped teaching and reprimanded us all. Then she pointed to me and said, "You over there cackling with your big mouth...." I remember feeling so deflated and humiliated. What this teacher did not realize was that I was getting teased about having full lips that same school year. Everyone in class laughed, and I felt so small. When I had time later and I was alone, my 5th grade self said to me, "You might not be prettier than everyone else, but you are, and will be, smarter than everyone else."

Perfectionism was born at that moment because I began to get validation from my grades and scores in school. Don't get me wrong, the great feeling of success from working hard should be celebrated. But, what I did not learn was that I was still acceptable and loved, even if I didn't get the grades. I carried that thought all the way into adulthood. I put so much pressure on myself to never "mess up." I learned to have anxiety, and it became an acceptable norm for me. I told myself that I should want to do everything to the best of my ability because who wants to be mediocre? In theory we should do our best, but will we ever do anything perfectly? NO, is the answer.

No one will ever be perfect at everything. And, frankly, what I learned was to embrace my imperfections as those are the things that make me unique. God created me to be different on purpose. Masterpieces are not masterpieces because they are done perfectly. Masterpieces are masterpieces because they are one of one. One of a kind. That's how God intended each of us to be. One of a kind, not perfect but moving in excellence with his help, of course. Some of the children in my 5th grade class may have teased me for having full lips, but I was created by God as one of a kind. There is no other Ari, and no one can be me. I was created with intention on purpose just the way I am, flaws and all.

In leadership, if you cannot accept your own flaws, you usually cannot tolerate anyone else's. How can you be an effective leader if no one can make a mistake around you? Now, making a mistake in my work was like the ultimate sin because as a nurse a mistake could cost a patient their life. In that context that would be terrible, but everything I needed to be at work did not apply to life outside of work. Ask yourself, do you bring your work home? Meaning do you bring home the mental requirements of your job home to your family, or have you learned to separate the two for balance? How will you assist those you are leading to have work-life balance if you don't have any? A great leader realizes they must lead themselves in a healthy way first before asking anyone else to follow. LeadHership starts within you, girl!

Who's Leading You?

In one of my first titled leadership positions, I was asked by my leader, "Where is your church home?" I answered him, and we continued our conversation and then after some time passed, I realized why he asked me that. When you are leading others, who is leading you? Who are you following that grounds the decisions you make and how you lead those on your team? Outside of the workplace it is what would be termed as your moral compass. What or who was I basing my moral compass on? I asked myself these questions as I was navigating how to lead myself and others.

I learned very quickly that it was a necessity to lean into my own personal relationship with God to make the best decisions and to gain the wisdom to navigate decision-making for myself and the team. Looking back, I see there were many times that I took unpopular positions that ultimately taught me to stand for what I believed in by sticking to my core value system while still honoring my place of employment. There was no way I accomplished that with my own strength. I quickly learned that I valued being able to look myself in the mirror each day knowing I did the very best I could and did not purposely harm another person. Sometimes that meant advocating for others over my own agenda because it was the right thing to do.

When we step on others for the sake of the task or to be considered successful, we slowly compromise parts of ourselves. Over time, the more compromises you make the more you lose of yourself. I watched many leaders lose themselves in their positions to save themselves, and in the end a very difficult lesson was learned. Stepping on others to achieve outcomes and success is not true happiness or success. At the end of the day, you still have to wake up with you and face yourself in the mirror each morning. What do you see when you look in the mirror?

Who Are You?

So many times in life we are faced with situations when we are asked to make decisions that may affect others. In my experience, the most difficult decision to make is when you realize those around you, or your place of employment, do not align with your personal value system and a critical decision has to be made. I faced this while working at an organization where the company's value system shifted from what I believed them to be. What I found out about myself during this time was that I had wrongly found my identity in the career that I had chosen. This doesn't sound like a bad thing right away since as a nurse you often hear that being a nurse is "a calling." I found myself in a leadership position advocating for employees who could not speak up for themselves. My upper management did not agree with what needed to happen to address the concerns these employees faced, and it did not align with my personal or professional values. I was so upset about this and could not understand how they could not see how important, pertinent, and legally necessary my concerns were.

What I learned was no matter how right you are, you cannot make anyone else value what you value, or see the potential dangers in their own decision-making if they are not open or receptive to change.

I also learned the value of knowing when to sever ties, whether with a person, or an organization. There are seasons for everything. I ended up having to make the decision to leave that organization and I was broken afterward. I lay on my couch unable to believe I had to leave an organization because advocating for employees' safety was flipped into an HR issue, and now my personality was on trial. I was BROKEN after realizing this job did not value what I brought to the table. Depression set in and eventually I came to the realization that I had found my identity in what I did in that position and that is the wrong mindset.

You must know your identity outside of your job description. Who are you without the accolades, degrees, certifications, and resume? Do you know you are more than what you do? Now looking back, I owe a big thank you to this organization because had they not misidentified me, I would not have found my true self again. I found out I am God's daughter. That I am redeemed in Christ. That grace and mercy follow me all the days of my life. That I am the head and never the tail. That I am more than any performance I could ever give or task I could accomplish. I challenge you, who are you outside of your job description? Who are you outside of what you are for others?

Be Brave!

As you grow and change, so too will your associations, positions, or places of employment. In our humanness, many times we want to hold on to everything due to our experiences. I was someone who wanted to hold on to every person and everything because I felt that I had lost so much in my life. Anxiety surrounded change, as it appeared negative to me. If you are reading this and you can relate, stop, and ask yourself, what new blessings are you holding up by holding on to people, places, or things that are no longer healthy for you for the sake of familiarity?

True growth is uncomfortable. If you stay in a place of familiarity and comfort all the time, how would you grow? It is often said that butterflies' wings get their strength by breaking out of the cocoon they were in as a caterpillar. Trials and challenges are gifts to us, really, so that we can see who we truly were created to be. Nothing we experience is a waste. It all makes the quilt of our life that is beautifully woven together and, in the end, serves the purpose. Even the worst of experiences are what make each of us unique and someone needs what you have learned.

BE BRAVE and let the world see all the amazing gifts inside of you.

Ari Wells

Ari Wells is the Owner and Founder of Levels of Freedom, LLC. Her mission is to empower women by helping them overcome self-limiting beliefs, boost self-confidence, and navigate starting over after life's challenges. At Levels of Freedom, our vision is to empower women to live the life they deserve full of purpose, joy, and fulfillment. Every woman has the right to walk boldly in her divine purpose and freedom. Ari is also the author of *"Girl You're Free! Shake Those Chains Off."*

Connect with Ari at www.levelsoffreedom.com.

CHAPTER 5

Mirroring Reflections: The Chrysalis

Banya Barua PhD

Cheers to the two men in my life - Vig and Venkat. The spirit and the wall without whom I would not be here recounting my story.

"Be yourself–not your idea of what you think somebody else's idea of yourself should be." ~Henry David Thoreau

---

Dressed in a suit befitting the role I had applied for, I was being interviewed for a senior consultant role in Sydney, Australia. The city I had relocated to following my husband's career move. Eight months into relocation, I had just about settled my son in his new primary school but had not yet adapted to the slow-paced life of a homemaker.

Leaving behind years of a fast-paced, solid career in human resources with an upward trajectory, it was quite a stretch to fit myself into the job search, tight-fisted monthly budgets, and reinventing myself as a full-time wife and mother, and also in my career. My role had been demanding; my mentor had planned a fast track designed to prepare me for senior management in five years in the global conglomerate that I worked in. At this juncture in my career, I had to leave behind all the career opportunities, change course, and relocate. Who does that? What kind of imprudent woman would leave a thriving career and practically commit a career suicide? Well, I had done it! And in all my senses. All for ensuring that my son did not suffer from being estranged from his father because how much ever you try, long distance and physically staying away from each other does cause discord in the family.

So here I was, attempting to restart my career. Building from scratch all over again. I was being interviewed for a role way below my capabilities and potential, but I needed a foot in the door. I had been advised by others who had experienced such relocation pain that I had to lie low, not highlight my strengths, and not sound strong and capable but rather be a person who can be molded and will be a good subordinate. I was counselled not to demonstrate any leadership qualities at all, as that would threaten my supervisor. So, I was doing my best to keep my capabilities under wrap and not reveal anything that might deter me from being hired. However much I tried, when the interviewer—who would have been my boss if I were hired, concluded the interview stating, "You could easily take my position," I knew that I had failed to present myself as the malleable subordinate material and the non-threatening candidate they were looking for.

This was not a new experience for me. The last 20 interviews that I had given had ended similarly, with interviewers quickly changing the tone of the interview after mentioning that I could easily take his/her position in the organization. On a personal note, I was even asked by one interviewer if I was pregnant, looking pointedly at my mid-section. I did not know how to react to such an observation and blurted out the truth that I was not pregnant. I was so taken aback by the sudden breach of privacy in the framing of the question that it did not occur to me to challenge it. It did not occur to me to point out that the interviewer was crossing the lines of privacy and decency. It was only after I reflected on my way home that I realized that he was searching for a reason to dismiss my candidature and would have used "my alleged pregnancy" as a justification for not acknowledging my candidature. The personal notes would have been used to find reasons to dismiss my candidature.

Reflecting upon these outcomes in trying to procure an appropriate job for myself, I realized that I could not hide my capabilities, skills, knowledge, experience, and personality, no matter how much I tried to. I could not hide my authentic self, and I am not good at masking myself. My reflection told me clearly that to build my future career, it is best to be as authentic as I can. The emphasis was on building my future career while being comfortable in my skin. For me, being authentic felt easy and simple. For me, being authentic and genuine seemed uncomplicated and noncontradictory to myself. It is better to accept myself for what I am and face all the challenges of living in a high-cost-of-living city like Sydney as a single-income family with multiple responsibilities to fulfill.

Thus began my journey of filling in the gaps in my personal development so I could match it with the capabilities, practical business knowledge, and depth of career experience I honed through the last 13 years of my career. The first thing I did was reassess my future plans. If I had been working in India, I would have initiated my plan of studying master's in management. So, I decided to begin my business education. I researched Sydney's universities. I was not an Australian citizen then, so I was not eligible for any governmental loans for higher education, which meant that I would have to use up my savings. It was a challenging undertaking to put at risk our financial security, especially when we were now a single-income family with three senior citizen dependents other than my son and me, depending on my husband's income. We were also supporting my sister, who lived in my residence in Bengaluru, working as a teacher. By lending her our Bengaluru home, we were giving her the fillip to embark on her life journey. My son, a six-year-old, had left his grandparents, a joint family, and a thriving social life in Bengaluru for a nuclear family setup with no friends and zero community support in Sydney. My child's situation implied that we needed to engage him in sports, music, and activities, adding expenses to our already tight financial situation. My husband was willing to take the risk of me studying full-time. With no friends, family, or community support in Sydney and limited liquidity, life was quite challenging, with psychological, mental, and finances stretched thin. All we had was us three for each other.

First of all, I joined the nearest university from home, 21 minutes by suburban train. The nearest university was the best choice as that would help me pick up and drop my son at the childcare without wasting a lot of time commuting. Not wasting time commuting was important since I did not want to be dependent on any neighbour, my son's or husband's friends, or any mothers that I had been introduced to as parents in the school community. Depending on new acquaintances means obligations and social obligations imply expenses denting savings. And we had to save even if it was as minimal as $500 a month. Even though my husband's salary was at par with the market rate, it would have been ample to live a comfortable life, even indulging in some luxuries. With so many dependents and in such foreign circumstances, healthy savings were unthinkable. We were living a THRIFTY life. Both financially and socially. This was a contrast to the lifestyle we were used to in

Bengaluru. The reason for opening up about my financial condition is to share my first reflection. ***The journey to authenticity begins at the minutest level, and the strength of authenticity lies in being aware of, acknowledging, and addressing the details. Including the unsavoury ones.***

The second step was stopping the use of cosmetics and my regular grooming sessions. Not indulging in salon treatments meant that my skin darkened. In a country where fairness was so vital, I took the risk of being judged for a dark complexion transformed beyond its natural skin tone. I stopped bothering about clothes and fashion. I practically lived in a pair of jeans, a Merino hoodie, and wedge-heeled boots. I tied up my hair so that I could tidy its unkemptness. Vanity was lost in my personal dictionary. A cursory look in the mirror was all the indulgence I gave myself. As long as I was clean, neat, and tidy I was satisfied with my bare minimum looks. I also started consciously working on my accent. Though I was advised by many, I did not want my environment to influence me to pick up a superficial and false Australian accent through imitation. Maintaining a strong awareness, I worked on developing a neutral accent and not being apologetic for my Indian accent. I decided I would rather keep my own accent than speak in an accent that belied my cultural origins. I risked being misjudged. I did try to improve to a neutral accent though. These insights mirror my second reflection. ***Authenticity begins from within***.

The third step was to choose companions who demonstrated like-mindedness, openness, and a nonjudgemental attitude with a growth mindset. Due to my family background, I am familiar with the Anglo-Saxon family and culture, which meant that I could relate to Australian Anglo-Saxon children and their parents. I also realized that I understood the multiple layers that made up the suburban community we were residing in. Without any haste, I made acquaintances. In

45

the meanwhile, I studied and concentrated on my son settling down at school and developing his social activities through sports and music. It was tough not to speak with anyone for days together. Light conversations and casual interactions were absolutely absent from my life. For me, learning to enjoy one's own companionship took a lot of patience, persistence, and a pragmatic approach, illustrating my third reflection. *Authenticity begins with self-awareness, reflection, and self-regulation.*

Thank goodness I was born into a Theravada Buddhist family. In these dire circumstances, I instinctively started meditating, a practice I had inherited from my grandmother. My childhood habit of practicing meditation helped me survive my lone journey into rediscovering my strengths, into studying in a new country, into studying with classmates who were not keen to befriend me as I could not socialize and party with them, being a primary child carer, I was time poor. Practicing meditation also helped me to self-regulate my emotions and not lose my emotional balance when my lecturers showed denigrating judgement of my profession in human resources. It was only when I started my doctoral studies five years later that self-analysis of my reflections told me that I was demonstrating grit. At that phase of my life, my instinctive practice of meditation in various forms, mindfulness, vipassana, pranayama, and yoga, revealed my fourth reflection. *To be authentic requires adopting a daily mind/intellectual training practice.*

Cogitating on the objective of living in the same style and manner that I was used to in Bengaluru became my goal. All I could think of was rejoining my career at the same trajectory where I had dropped it. My passion for regaining my career, securing my finances, and leading the same lifestyle or even improving my lifestyle drove me. My husband was regularly travelling for work, which left my little child and me alone. Did I feel scared? Yes, I did feel scared. But I did not succumb to the feelings of loneliness, worry, or fear. If ever I felt these emotions, I would shake them off. I would remind myself of my objective and strengthen my resolve. I did not want to feel obligated to my new acquaintances, nor did I want them to feel that I was making friends to fulfill a self-centered purpose, so turning to anyone was not possible for me. Every time I failed to meet my expectations; I wrote it down. Simple things like not being able to walk fast enough to the station to catch the train that would reach 10 minutes before my son's after-school care /tennis class closed. At the same time, when I achieved something I wanted, I rejoiced and rewarded myself. It could be as simple as being able to draft my assignments a week before submission and complete two more drafts of the submission before the due date. The amalgamation of these small steps of mine elucidates my fifth reflection. *To be authentic requires being objective, pragmatic, and true to one's strengths and weaknesses, creating achievable milestones.*

By this time, we had spent six years in Sydney. These six years were an exile for me. Sometimes I imagined myself as a butterfly. That butterfly was going through the chrysalis stage of transforming from a caterpillar. Now, we relocated to Melbourne. My life changed positively. I founded my consulting firm and also started my doctoral candidature. Did my struggles end? No, they did not. However, I was better equipped to begin my journey as an academician and a founder. I started earning regularly. I started developing my circle of friends. My social circle developed. Life did not become easy, but it became manageable. I learnt to predict my weaknesses. I learnt to generally foresee situations and let go of control where I could not wield influence. I learnt to trust and build trust. I learnt that my inherent self was sufficient, and I did not have to rely on anything that was cosmetic or superficial. I learnt the value of time. I learnt the value of silence. I learnt that whatever life threw at me, it was my response that shaped the outcome. I learnt that I did not have to respond to everything. I learnt to trust. I learnt to trust myself and the inherent goodness in others. I learnt that my attitude, my conduct, and my behaviour play a pivotal role in shaping my life. I learnt that I am comfortable with my vulnerabilities. Being authentic helped me develop genuine friendships that are nurturing and caring, become resilient, strengthen my journey to self-sufficiency, and achieve my goals through grit – passion, and perseverance while being brutally honest to myself about myself all the time, acknowledging help and appreciating support received. ***Being authentic helped me attract genuine people, nurture strong relationships, create teams, develop collaborations, build projects, and sustain business while being servant, ethical, adaptable, collaborative, and transformational in my approach to working with people.***

What did I have to overcome? I overcame the feelings of being daunted from revealing my authentic self. Being transparent was hard. I had to overcome the ignorance I found hidden in me, revealing that I was unaware of the contradictions in my behaviours and actions. I worried about not being able to please everyone or not being able to be in the good books of everyone I wanted. I did not want to risk my relationships. I was wary of the creepy crawlies that may start coming out of the cracks in my relations, marring the relationship equations. At the beginning of the transformation, I had misunderstood authenticity as being positive about everything, whether that includes being superficial, contradictory, or even hypocritical in my responses and actions. I had to rethink that being diplomatic requires compromising their authenticity. I experienced that being authentic upsets the prevalent patriarchal system and does not fulfill the expectations of the prevalent patriarchal system. Initially, my sense of vulnerability made me insecure about my authenticity. Today, as a leadership development researcher and coach, these revelations help me attune with my clients helping them to delve deep into themselves to discover their inherent authenticity and learn to apply it in their daily lives to become authentic leaders in their own right.

Through my recount, I share my experience of my transformation into an authentic leader and my gains from being an authentic leader. I also share strategies on how I developed into an authentic leader. In a nutshell, my experiences reflect that adopting authenticity is tough, but the result is enriching. Developing authenticity is challenging, but once attained, sustaining and managing authenticity is simple, easy, and smooth. Being detail-oriented, self-aware, self-regulated, reflecting, practicing daily mind /intellectual training, objective, pragmatic, true to one's strengths and weaknesses, and creating achievable milestones with grit and resilience are required to develop authenticity. The outcome of authenticity is trust, transparency, genuine relationships, a wide scope of growth, sustainable collaborations, profitable business, and a thriving life.

Banya Barua PhD

Researching leadership, gender, and workplace well-being, Banya Barua has presented papers at international conferences, conducted workshops, and published articles and chapters on the application of workplace well-being programs and leadership development. As a social scientist, she is comfortable using qualitative, quantitative, and mixed methodologies and is an adept and empathetic interviewer.

She applies her corporate experience in the Information and Technology industry to teach courses on Strategic Human Resources, Workplace Well-being, and People Analytics and in her passion for research. She associates with the academic institutions as an adjunct. She lends her expertise to people's behaviours, skills, and attitudes.

Banya founded EsseMC Pty Ltd – a research-based management consultancy specializing in workplace well-being and corporate mindfulness integrating her research areas with her specialization and special interests in strategic human resources, leadership studies, human-centric issues with technology, and women at work.

In her corporate life, Dr. Banya Barua coaches to develop leaders and mentors Generation Z to develop their full potential and achieve success. She has experience in designing curriculum and assessment, developing content, and creating courses. Having worked in management she leads with agility, authenticity, and creativity. She uses project management and "design thinking" skills to initiate and implement programs. Some of the previous projects impacted 2000-3000 people. In these years, she collaborated with diverse businesses, operations, and functions of HR while partnering with business units to fulfill her role and responsibilities. She has exposure to multicultural diverse work environments having worked across the US, UK, APAC, and India.

Connect with Banya at www.essemc.com.

CHAPTER 6

The Strong-Willed Child
That Became a Leader

Brenda Siri

---

*This chapter is dedicated to my late mother, Ramona, who
demanded I be a straight A student and
strong female leader.*

---

s the path to leadership a choice, or is it something natural that happens
to those who were designated as "strong-willed children"? I was the
youngest of four children in my family. My three siblings were much
older than me and had a different father. He died tragically while driving
home from work one evening, leaving my mother to raise a 16-year-old
boy and girls ages 14 and nine-years-old. Soon after, my mother met
my father, remarried, and had me.

My personality has always been different from that of my siblings. I walked at 8 months and ran around the house in my mother's high heels by nine months. In the 1960s, there were no laws stating how old you had to be to start school. If you were smart enough, you could go. My mother put me into a prestigious private school in San Diego where I was the youngest kindergartener ever. I have always excelled at academia.

As a child, I played school with all my dolls. I loved education so much, that at just nine years old I asked my church pastor if I could teach Sunday school. I didn't get the job, but I wanted it. I wanted to lead and share my knowledge. This felt natural to me, even as a young girl. I didn't understand it then, but from a young age being a mentor and a leader was something that I had inside me.

At the ripe old age of 15, I had completed school and was ready to go to college. I told my mother I wanted to become a schoolteacher. She told me no. She said she would not pay for me to go to college to get a degree that would pay me nothing. She wasn't wrong, but what a shame that our society has deemed education as a career one chooses because it is their passion and not because it pays the bills.

My mother told me I was good at math. I won math awards at school. In the 10th grade, I was allowed to be a math tutor for the 9th grade algebra students. See, I finally got my chance to "teach," and all my mother got out of it was that I was a good math student. She decided I would get a college degree in accounting to become an accountant. Being 15 years old, I didn't really have a choice. I had to listen to her. So off we went to college. My parents drove me from California to Texas, where I attended a Christian university to become an accountant.

After one year in college, and becoming a licensed driver, my mother realized she didn't like having her 16-year-old daughter 1,300 miles from home. So as fast as I was driven to Texas to attend school,

I was unenrolled and driven back home. My mother decided that business college was a better option for me, and she enrolled me in a local business school where I could go during the day and be home for dinner. In business school, I learned some fundamentals of accounting, how to type (probably the most valuable skill I received), and took some business English classes. At the end of the nine-month program, I was ready to become... an Office Manager!

I got my first job the way almost everyone did in the early '80s. I read the newspaper. I looked through ads and started making phone calls to see who would allow me to come speak with them. As you can imagine, I was now only 17 years old, but I was a very mature 17-year-old. I was under no obligation to tell anyone how old I was when I went for interviews. I just represented myself well. I got a job working for a mortgage company as their receptionist. I was good at it because I was well-spoken and friendly. From there, my career skyrocketed into Office Management. I loved this role, because it allowed me to interact with all of the employees, make sure that we had office supplies, do the filing, and make the coffee. What I didn't know is that this was the path to human resources.

In the early 1980s, companies didn't have large human resources departments. Typically, the owners of the company oversaw all aspects of human resources, until the birth of human resource management in the 1980s. Within a year, the mortgage company gave me more responsibility. I was now responsible for loan processing, payroll, accounts payable, accounts receivable, and the hiring of new employees. It was so time-consuming that I was allowed to hire my first employee.

My administrative assistant was young. She had only been a medical receptionist and had no experience with computers. I would have to teach her a few things, but I loved teaching. I hired her based on a gut feeling. I just really liked her and thought that we would work well together. I guess that even back then, I realized that the office culture could contribute to the success of a working relationship. In the beginning, I took a scared young girl and taught her how to use a computer. I had to teach her how to use the programs that would help her do her job. I loved it. I finally felt like my career was taking me down a path I was supposed to be on. I was now being paid to be a leader and a mentor. I was responsible for helping someone else be successful.

I left that job after three years. I had outgrown it. I was hungry for bigger challenges. And I left the owner of the company with a highly trained administrative assistant who was ready to step in and take over my job. She and I still talk today, and she told me recently that my guidance and teaching helped her thrive in her position for the next three years. From there, she also grew in her career, and she credits me with her career success because of the mentoring, guidance, teaching, and leadership, I gave her almost 30 years ago.

After leaving my first job, I went to work for one of the largest general contractors in northern California. I became a project assistant at a $50 million dollar hospital building. I put on my jeans, boots, and a hard hat and sat on a construction site every day. I loved it. I was one of very few women in a male-dominated world. But they all showed me respect, and allowed me to be a leader for the office team. In just one year, I was stollen away from another general contractor company who allowed me to get out of the field and into the office. I was now an official member of the human resources department.

I was told by the President of the company that I was a natural. I was good at developing processes and procedures. I was, and still am, highly organized. I was seen as a good listener, who could give constructive feedback. I was told that I was a force to be reckoned with, while maintaining empathy in the process. I still had a very strong gut instinct about people and was not afraid to hire or fire anyone. The President nicknamed me "the terminator" because they called me into any manager's office who needed to let someone go for performance reasons. And, yes, I had to be there to deliver the news.

Being "the terminator" taught me a lot as a business professional. I didn't like to see people get fired. I didn't like knowing that the words coming out of my mouth made a huge difference in their well-being, and their livelihood. It hurt and felt painful to me. I decided to try and find a more positive route to be in human resources without having to fire people. I wanted to be on the happy side of human resources. The one where people are grateful to be getting a job. It wasn't called talent acquisition back then. But whatever it was, I liked that side of human resources much more.

My friend worked for an employment agency and Monster had just come onto the scene. This new tool allowed people to apply for jobs using a computer. No one had to come to a job site and fill out a paper application. The world of hiring talent was becoming more sophisticated, and I wanted to be part of it. I talked with my friend, and we took the plunge together to start our own agency. With her external knowledge of hiring and my internal corporate knowledge of hiring, we felt we could provide outstanding solutions for our clients. I took on the role of business development. I went out and knocked on doors, got the trust of businesses to hire us to help them fill their roles. And we did. We built a successful business that lasted for two years until she decided to move away. Alone, I didn't trust I could do it. So, we closed the business.

From there, I went back to school. I wanted the college degree I never finished. I still loved academia and learning, and now I had a better grasp on who I wanted to be professionally. I got my bachelor's degree in business and continued in the world of talent acquisition for other companies. I worked with agencies for years before starting another agency myself. I had great success for a couple of years, before a headhunter called me and asked me to consider going back to the corporate world. I was reluctant, until I met the leadership team and the team I would manage. The timing felt right. Managing a team of recruiters at a national technology firm, I found a real passion. I loved leading others and sharing my years of knowledge with them. As a leader, I never told my team that they worked FOR me. They worked WITH me. Our role was to find the best talent to be part of the company. This was the happy side of human resources, until I had to make difficult decisions about my own team.

The terminator was back. I had some underperformers and some employees who wanted to try different aspects of human resources. So I let them fly and go into other parts of the department to learn new skills. I would never hold someone back. I wanted my team to feel fulfilled by their work. As the company grew, so did my team. And as I hired new recruiters, I allowed my team to be part of the recruiting and selection process. I wanted a team that had a good cultural fit, and so we made choices together about each new person we brought to the talent acquisition team. I also tried a new approach to organizing my team by building silos.

Most of my team had been in a recruiting function for at least 5 years. Some really knew what they were best at and felt they had a specialization. I agreed and allowed them to only fill roles that applied to their specific area of specialization. For those who were unsure, we worked together to determine what field of work they were most interested in. And if they were unsure, they got to try recruiting for anything and everything until we found their passion. I wanted my team to feel like they could have a career in recruiting with direction, and so I built a path for each of them to follow.

After a number of years in corporate recruiting and going back to school to obtain my master's degree, I was given the opportunity to become an adjunct professor for the University of Texas at Dallas, teaching professional development to international students. I made it! I finally got to teach school and be called Professor Siri. What an honor this was when the opportunity arose. And it has been nothing short of that since. It is truly the most humbling role I have ever had. And my mother, who passed in 2018, would likely be very proud of me for achieving my goal.

I also knew it was time to get out of corporate recruiting and return to what I loved most. I went back to being an agency recruiter, and back to my own company, where I have been ever since and where I plan to stay. My company, Corporate Connections LLC, was founded in 2015, and I rejoined the company in 2022 as the President and CEO. The company has flourished and grown in many ways. We have a talented team of recruiters who help me find the best of the best for my clients. My approach to talent acquisition is quite different for my clients and it is something I expect from my team when it comes to providing strong talent to our clients. Our white glove approach means that no candidate will be put in front of a client without being fully vetted. We ask the right questions to assess the talent of the candidates we speak with. And we provide those interview notes to our clients, so they can make educated decisions as to whether or not to interview a candidate.

My leadership philosophy has not changed over the years. I had a vision for Corporate Connections LLC, and I knew that my efforts and goals meant a lot of hard work. I knew it meant putting my strength as a coach and mentor into building a team that would help the company be successful. I try to be extremely uplifting to my team. I try to encourage them to achieve their own goals and objectives for success. I am not just managing the organization and making the decisions, I am working daily to inspire those who work with me, so that together we can all be successful.

The success of my organization is based on solid communication. The way we communicate with our clients, or candidates, and each other means that there is always clarity in the vision. Our clients don't have to wonder if we are working on their open positions. Our candidates don't have to wonder if they will hear from us about a job they applied for. And our team never has to worry about asking questions. I lead others to watch them grow and be successful. And it all starts with ensuring that those I work with in any capacity know that they can come to me at any time. My career has allowed me to be everything I wanted to be as a child — a mentor, a coach, a teacher, and a leader.

Brenda Siri

Brenda Siri is a global Human Resources and Talent executive with over 20 years of experience. Brenda brings a trusting style that has facilitated the ability to build relationships and provide an open and collaborative culture. She is currently the President and CEO of Corporate Connections LLC, a global HR and talent acquisition consulting firm. She and her firm were featured as Top 10 Influential Entrepreneur to be inspired by.

Brenda has a diverse professional background, working for global organizations like Booz, Allen & Hamilton, Korn Ferry, and Citigroup. She has also supported private equity, mid-size, and startup technology organizations. She has a bachelor's degree in Business and a master's degree in Organizational Management, with a minor in Organizational Leadership where she graduated Summa cum laude. In addition, Brenda is also an Adjunct Professor for The University of Texas at Dallas, where she teaches Professional Development to international master's degree students. Sharing her passion for people and talent acquisition, Brenda instills the skills necessary to help students obtain internship and full-time job opportunities.

Brenda is also on the Board of Women with Promise, a non-profit organization that offers educational scholarships to women currently residing in shelters due to abuse or sex trafficking circumstances. Her passion for helping those in need is evidenced by her ability to support the organization's fundraising efforts.

Connect with Brenda at www.corporateconnectionsllc.com.

CHAPTER 7

Roots of Resilience: Leadership Lessons from Immigrant Parents

Cecilia Dahl

Dedicated to my parents.

It was Christmas of 1967, and the air in Bergen, Norway, carried the sharp sting of winter, crisp, and biting against the skin. The cold seemed to hang in the air, almost palpable, as the faint scent of pine and wood smoke mingled with the fresh, frosty breeze. Inside a cozy house on the outskirts of the city, warmth radiated from every corner. The flickering candles cast a soft glow on the faces of a group of young adults, all in their early twenties, united by their shared history.

These young adults were born in the tumultuous era of World War II, emerging into a world shrouded in the darkness of Nazi occupation. Growing up in the aftermath of conflict, their formative years were etched with the indelible lessons of survival, resilience, and the painstaking process of reconstruction. Now, as they stood on the precipice of adulthood, they were not merely poised to enter the world; they were ready to forge their own paths, armed with the courage, and tenacity that defined their generation.

Among them was my father, Jarle. At 25, he was already dreaming of a future far beyond the borders of Norway. While most of his friends were settling into studies and careers, content to remain close to the fjords and mountains that had shaped their childhoods, Jarle's heart was elsewhere. He had long known that Norway wasn't his future. His dreams had once led him to consider Australia, but over time, his ambitions settled firmly on America. It wasn't a question of whether he would go — it was only a matter of when.

Across the room sat Sissel, my mother, quietly observing the lively scene. At 24, she lived in Oslo, training to become a librarian, and had returned home for Christmas. She hadn't planned on attending the party but was persuaded by her cousin to attend. She didn't know many people there, but that didn't matter. In the midst of all the celebration, one face stood out — Jarle. When their eyes met, something sparked between them.

After that night, life returned to its usual rhythm. Sissel went back to her studies in Oslo, and Jarle continued preparing for his journey to America. They met only once more in the months that followed. Time wasn't on their side, and the possibility of something more between them seemed slim. Yet, even with only two encounters to build on, Jarle knew he couldn't leave without one final leap of faith. He invited Sissel for a weekend of skiing in the mountains with the intent of starting a life together.

In the crisp air of the Norwegian plateau, Jarle proposed. It was a moment of profound decision for both of them. If she said no, their story would end before it truly began. But if she said yes, they would embark on an extraordinary adventure — leaving behind everything they had ever known to start a life together in a foreign land. Sissel said yes, and in that instant, they committed not only to each other but to a life of uncertainty, resilience, and courage.

This decision would set the foundation for the life they would build and the lessons they would unknowingly pass on to their children. True leadership, I've come to realize, often begins at the edge of your comfort zone, where courage is tested, and bold decisions redefine your path. My parents, without intending to, taught me some of the most profound lessons about leadership — not through formal titles or corporate structures, but through their everyday choices, especially the ones that required them to step into the unknown.

Although I wasn't born when they made that leap, their story has been a guiding example throughout my life. They showed me that leadership isn't always about grand gestures or leading teams. Sometimes, it's about the quiet, personal decisions that shape our lives and the courage to take risks when the future is uncertain. Their decision to marry and start a new life in America, even though they barely knew each other, was a perfect example of this kind of quiet leadership.

Life in America wasn't easy, especially for my mother. My father, through his school, quickly found himself surrounded by classmates who made the transition more bearable. My mother, on the other hand, had no such network. As an immigrant in a foreign land, she struggled with homesickness, and the isolation that came with being far from the familiar. She missed Norway, her friends, her family, and the life she had left behind. The strain of starting over in a strange country began to weigh heavily on her, and at times, she considered returning home.

It was during one of these low moments that she confided in my father, expressing her unhappiness, and her thoughts of returning to

Norway. His response would become a turning point in her life. He told her, "I want you to be happy, and I'll support you in whatever you decide. But your happiness — that's something only you can take responsibility for."

Those words, though simple, sparked a profound realization in my mother. Happiness wasn't something that could be given to her — it had to be something she created for herself. She couldn't expect my father or anyone else to bear the responsibility for her fulfillment. From that moment on, my mother made a conscious decision to take ownership of her happiness. She began to carve out her own space in their new life, building a sense of fulfillment that was independent of my father, but not without his support.

Early in my career, I often felt responsible for 'fixing' people's problems. I would try to do everything myself, seeing it as my duty to smooth the path for those I led. It was my default mode, one that gave me a sense of control and purpose. But over time, I realized that leadership is about empowering others to navigate their own challenges. Just as my father encouraged my mother to take responsibility for her happiness, I learned that supporting my team to find their own solutions — whether resolving conflicts or overcoming obstacles — created a stronger, more resilient dynamic. This shift transformed not only my leadership but also the success of those I worked with, allowing them to grow in ways they couldn't if I had simply stepped in.

My parents' challenges didn't end there. Living in South Dakota, my mother had to build a new community from scratch. She found work at the local library, where she was often the only immigrant in a sea of locals who had known each other for years. Though she spoke English fluently, her accent marked her as an outsider. "Fitting in was the hardest part of the move," my mom would say. Fitting in was difficult, and at times, she felt the weight of being different in a place where everyone seemed to belong.

One of her coworkers, Elsie, held negative views about Native Americans, views that my mother found deeply troubling. My mom disagreed with many of Elsie's opinions, yet she understood that trying to change someone's mindset was often a fruitless endeavor. Instead of allowing their differences to create tension, she chose a more constructive path. She focused on working with Elsie, emphasizing her strengths, and contributions rather than dwelling on the areas where they clashed. She often told me, "You can respect people for their skills, even if you don't agree with everything they think or say." This approach required a level of emotional intelligence that my mom had honed over the years.

This was another subtle leadership lesson my parents taught me: leadership is about finding strength in diversity. Early in my career, I struggled with this. I approached disagreements defensively, eager to protect my own views rather than genuinely listening to others. I hadn't yet grasped the power of opening my mind with real curiosity, to value perspectives different from my own. Over time, I learned that embracing an all-sides view was transformational not only for me but also for my team. This shift allowed me to lead with empathy and true openness — a lesson I pass on today, especially to leaders of remote teams. When leaders embrace diversity in all its forms, they unlock a powerful asset that fosters innovation, trust, and unity, even across distances.

As my parents continued to navigate their new life in America, they faced another challenge — their own relationship. Considering they had barely known each other when they decided to embark on this journey together, it's not surprising that their early years of marriage were marked by tension, particularly over finances. My father controlled most of the money, which created friction between them.

The tension in our home during those early years felt almost tangible, like the air itself was thick with unresolved conflict. I couldn't escape the sound of their frustration, the sharp, cutting exchanges that often seemed to have no end. It wasn't just the noise, though; it was the feeling that settled over everything — a sense of instability that lingered long after the shouting stopped. I never fully understood what sparked these frequent blowouts, but I knew money was always at the heart of it.

Then, one day almost without warning, the storm in our house quieted. The constant friction that had once filled the rooms seemed to dissolve, and an unfamiliar calm took its place. Life smoothed itself out. It wasn't until years later that I learned what had shifted between them — during that final blowout, they realized they had to make a change and decided to share responsibility for finances. This choice transformed my parents' marriage, easing the tensions that had threatened to pull them apart.

The key to that peace was my father's realization that sharing responsibility didn't mean losing control. He learned to trust my mother, to empower her to make decisions and take ownership. This shift in how they worked together brought balance to their relationship, and with it, peace to our home. Looking back, it was one of the more profound lessons I ever learned about leadership: leadership isn't about holding tight to control — it's about trusting those around you to step up and share the load.

This choice transformed my parents' marriage, easing the tensions that had threatened to pull them apart. I saw echoes of their journey in my own experience as a headstrong founder. In the early days of my first startup, I was a force of nature — relentless and driven, pushing forward with a single-minded focus on reaching our goals. It was a vulnerable time for the business, and I often believed that success rested solely on my shoulders. Looking back, I realize I was often intimidating, a whirlwind of energy that left little room for others to step in. But over time, like my father, I learned the value of letting go and sharing the load. I discovered that true strength in leadership lies in trusting others to rise to the challenge, creating a space where everyone can bring their unique skills and perspectives to the table. This shift brought out the best in my team and fostered a culture of shared responsibility and growth.

As I reflect on the lessons I've learned from my parents, I realize how deeply their experiences have influenced my understanding of leadership. Their journey was far from smooth — marked by challenges, disagreements, and moments of uncertainty. They weren't reading leadership books or attending seminars, but through their everyday struggles, they were teaching me powerful lessons about what true leadership looks like.

It isn't about holding a position of authority or making every decision. Instead, they showed me that leadership is rooted in courage — the bravery to face difficult situations head-on — and resilience — the ability to keep going, even when things feel overwhelming. They demonstrated trust, not just in each other but in the people around them, and they embraced collaboration, understanding that two minds working together are stronger than one trying to carry the load alone. These values — courage, resilience, trust, and collaboration — are the very foundation of the leadership I aspire to today.

In today's fast-paced, digitally connected world, where leadership often takes place from behind a screen, the ability to trust, and empower others has become absolutely essential. With teams spread across different locations and time zones, leaders must rely on their ability to delegate responsibilities, foster autonomy, and build strong relationships from a distance. The success of leading teams in remote workspaces hinges on creating an environment where individuals feel trusted and supported to take ownership of their work, even when they are miles apart. Empowering others in this way not only strengthens team dynamics but also drives innovation, accountability, and resilience in an increasingly virtual landscape.

In these dispersed work environments, developing leadership skills requires deliberate effort — purposeful interactions, intentional mentorship, and a strong emphasis on building trust.

Leadership is happening all around us, in moments big, and small. I witnessed my father's determination as he navigated the complexities of starting over, embracing the unknown with resilience and optimism. Simultaneously, my mother's quest for fulfillment in a foreign culture revealed the strength of self-discovery and adaptability. Their experiences taught me that leadership isn't confined to formal titles or positions of authority; it emerges from the choices we make in the face of uncertainty.

Inspired by the courage my parents showed in moving to a foreign land, I too embraced risk throughout my career. I took on new jobs, launched ventures, and pushed myself beyond comfort zones, seeing each challenge as an opportunity to grow stronger. As my own leadership evolved, I realized that true leadership isn't about being at the front of the pack. It's about standing beside, and sometimes behind, those you lead. I began to view myself as a coach, a support structure rather than a solitary figurehead. By letting go and embracing the genius and power of others, I witnessed the transformation not only in my business but also in the growth and success of those I led. This shift fostered a culture where every voice mattered, driving innovation, unity, and resilience.

As I forge ahead on my own journey, I embrace these invaluable lessons, recognizing that leadership is not defined by perfection, but by the willingness to navigate uncharted territories with grace, to cultivate trust among those around me, and to embrace the learning process that comes with each challenge.

In this ever-evolving landscape of leadership, I remain committed to growth and adaptation, understanding that each experience is an opportunity for insight and evolution. I carry with me the understanding that leadership is a continuous journey of self-discovery and empowerment, both for myself, and for those I have the privilege to work with. Ultimately, it is this blend of vulnerability and courage that lays the foundation for impactful leadership, inspiring not only personal growth but also a collective commitment to excellence in every endeavor.

Cecilia Dahl

Cecilia Dahl is a passionate entrepreneur, speaker, author, and two-time Stevie Award winner for Women in Business. As a recognized thought leader and advocate for the future of work, Cecilia empowers companies to harness the full potential of remote teams through intentional leadership, fostering engagement, and inspiring a shared sense of purpose. Founder of The Remote Leadership Lab, Cecilia draws from her journey of growing Smart Destinations into a hundred-million-dollar enterprise, where she discovered that distance is no barrier to connection, collaboration, or success.

Leading remote teams requires a new level of intentionality—every action, every message, and every connection must be purposeful. Cecilia knows that for remote teams to thrive, it's no longer a choice but an imperative to equip managers at all levels with the skills and tools to lead effectively. This intentional practice in leadership, she believes, is the foundation for building cohesive, collaborative, and deeply engaged teams.

Through speaking, consulting, and The Remote Leadership Lab, Cecilia helps leaders turn this vision into reality, transforming teams into resilient, purpose-driven communities that embody what she calls "Remote Remarkable"—where dedication to the mission and to each other thrives, no matter the distance.

Connect with Cecilia at www.RemoteLeadershipLab.com.

CHAPTER 8

Awakening to My Inner Truth

Emiliana Molina Fajardo

Mom, dad, thank you for your unconditional love and patience through my growing pains. Cami, Andre, thank you for trying your best to understand me and wishing I get to "have it all." May we always continue to be here for each other. With love to my family in Colombia.

March 15, 2022—Departing from Fort Lauderdale-Hollywood International Airport

My heart is racing as I'm running to get a second COVID test done at the Fort Lauderdale-Hollywood International Airport. In the midst of my anxiety, I notice I'm holding my breath and am feeling overwhelmed by all the paperwork I need to complete before I travel to Israel and Egypt. A third test is required upon arrival in Tel Aviv. My patience is thinning. My inner sacred rebel is screaming: "Agh! I'm not good at following systemic structure," and here I am, trying my best. And then I hear the voice of my inner angel calming my nerves: "I'm learning to plan ahead and it's not easy for someone like me—a creative artist at heart, who's more comfortable with a flow state than strict structure." I breathe as I have this realization and then my inner wise Guru just says: "You've got this."

Boarding the first flight, the face mask is getting in my way—it's stifling. I rarely wear it. It irritates me. I feel enraged that we're being forced to hinder our ability to breathe through a face mask by a baseless theory that—I intuitively knew—would later be debunked by science and hearings in Capitol Hill in Washington D.C. One of my teachers at Northwestern University once told me I was a natural at predicting future outcomes and stories that were "newsworthy." She recognized back then a gift I wasn't aware of. My intuition and my ability to see hidden truths; a talent I would begin to strengthen and nurture on this trip.

I was learning and growing with what seemed like the most mundane scenario. I could feel the promise of a rewarding spiritual journey as I began to find my seat on the plane. I quickly began to see the signs from my angels and the Egyptian Goddess of truth, balance and cosmic order, Ma'at. I could feel her guidance and embrace as shivers moved through my spine, up my arms—an extension of my heart—I was experiencing my soul's expansion. My Angels were with me every step of the way. I was getting to know myself all over again.

I found my seat on the plane and began to reflect on the last three years of my life, when everything crumbled to pieces. I used to unconsciously choose to learn through pain and suffering and the more I got to know myself, I realized I could choose to grow through love, joy and grace. While sitting in window seat 17F, looking at the instruction pamphlets with the number 737, I started to connect the signs. I was being guided to look up the meaning of angel number 777. I surrendered in my seat as we began to take off. It felt like my dark night of the soul—that began in 2019—when I was a former White House correspondent in Washington D.C. covering Trump's administration, and as I was going through a divorce in 2020, was coming to an end.

My aunt, Carmenza Molina, was a core pillar in my spiritual awakening. She held me through my divorce in 2020 as I told my ex-husband I had cheated on him. Some people called me "stupid" for telling him and others applauded my courage. As I looked out the small airplane window, I recognized that speaking my heart's truth was the right choice for me. I strengthened my integrity and felt much lighter living a life in transparency.

By speaking my truth, I gave him the choice to stay or to leave knowing the full spectrum of my vulnerabilities, my mistakes and my humanness. After this heartbreak, I understood I had spent so much of my life believing that pain was the only teacher. I've been so hard on myself—especially after my divorce; my inner judge and self-punishment were brutal. I cheated. I hurt someone I loved. I learned that love is a choice and we're constantly growing, getting to know ourselves and our partner. I learned that healthy relationships require you to respect your partner's free will and their chosen experiences. It's a path that leads us to our ultimate freedom when we have courageous conversations. A partnership requires loving ourselves to find our freedom in relation to each other. Sometimes this means you have to be willing to face the fear of losing your loved one before losing yourself.

The "right" partner will love you so deeply, this love will continuously set you free. This love will feel expansive; not contracted. We're all human and we came to learn and we don't get to decide how others experience their life and growth. We can only do what feels in integrity with our hearts and honoring the agreements we made with each other as best we can.

Seeking support in 2020, I immersed myself in the world of angels. My aunt initiated my path to become an Angelic Healer (one of the many miracles that flourished from the pain). I began to write about my trip and document everything I was experiencing, all the thoughts that were surfacing and all the emotions that were seeking the light as tears fell down my cheeks. I could feel I was being guided by a higher purpose within and all I had to do was surrender and trust the journey. As my thoughts continued to flutter through my head, the flight took off.

March 16, 2022—Arriving in Tel Aviv, Israel

"Brucheem," or "welcome" in Hebrew (it can also be used to say "blessed"), was the first sign I encountered as I landed in the Ben Gurion International Airport in the outskirts of Tel Aviv. Google translator became my best friend since seeing the foreign language felt overwhelming and exciting. I breathed deeply as I landed on this sacred land.

Last and third COVID test upon entering Israel, "thank God," I think to myself as I get past my annoyance with the procedures. I couldn't handle another Q-tip violating my nostrils. I passed all the tests to begin the joyful part of the adventure. Or so I thought.

I quickly found a taxi and headed out to meet my cousin, Cristina, and her husband, Alejandro. They were living in Tel Aviv for a year and that became the perfect excuse for me to visit. The taxi driver, with a strong accent, stated the initial fare to take me to their apartment on Bograshov Street, two blocks away from the Beach.

He hands me a receipt that states all fares are strictly charged by the meter. Yet, the meter isn't on. This feels like a test. Being born in Medellin, Colombia, I know better. We endured violence, theft and scams in the '90s and I felt like my voice had often been silenced due to fear of conflict.

We were 10 minutes into the journey, and I silently asked my angels to fill him with light to protect me from all ill intent. Immediately, I felt his attitude shift, he lowered the fare for me, and I silently let out a huge sigh of relief.

I was finding it easier to speak my truth. I used to let my emotions build up and I would respond with anger or irritability. This led to escalated conflicts back then and I don't feel proud of those reactions. I've learned that behind my anger there was a profound grief that needed to be acknowledged. My anger was always valid and justified; my response to certain situations–were not.

I had so much shame and guilt built up from past situations. My cousin, Sebastian, once told me, "guilt does not exist." Guilt is the emotion we feel in the present moment, thanks to our mistakes from the past, with the wisdom we have today.

We arrived at the apartment and I paid the driver 116 shekels by credit card and (seeing the displeasure on his face) I gave him an additional $40. I learned to research the cost of a local taxi to avoid getting ripped off; never rush into agreements and to honor my word with initial verbal agreements. All that wisdom just from a taxi drive, "Phew! Who knew."

March 17, 2022—Tel Aviv, Israel

I arrived during Purim, a Jewish holiday that celebrates the story of the Jewish people's deliverance from a planned genocide in ancient Persia. Everyone was dressed up in costumes and my cousin and her husband took me out dancing to celebrate. I couldn't sleep when we got back. I was lying on the couch in my cousin's apartment in Tel Aviv, listening to music, looking out the window, and from a little corner of the balcony, between a tree, I could perfectly see the almost-full moon. I began to speak to it.

The song, *"Tejiendo Alas"* by Malú, started to play. It means "weaving wings." And I felt the moon was speaking to me through the lyrics of that song. I began to shed tears, feeling the moon's embrace, helping me release my fears. It had been two years since the divorce, and I was still grieving and finding comfort in nature, spirituality and family. (It's interesting how life works in ways to mirror back to you the gaps in your inner work.) I have been on both sides of the coin in relationships. I've been cheated on and I've cheated. A woman's intuition and sixth sense never fail her. Both sides of the coin hurt equally as bad, and truthfully it was much more painful for me to recognize that I had acted out of integrity with my values, my essence and our vows than the act of cheating itself.

March 23, 2022—Arriving in Cairo, Egypt

"Shakira, Shakira," the Egyptian salesmen would playfully scream at me as I walked past the markets. I guess that's what Egyptians call most Latinas when they see someone who looks like me. I enjoyed the compliment and external validation that was empowering me to rebuild my self-esteem; even if it was a white lie to try to sell me their art.

I landed in Cairo, Egypt, and met up with my tour guide and my group for the next adventure; we would be exploring all the temples and climbing Mount Sinai, where Moses received the Ten Commandments.

The streets were crowded, the cars were honking, and there were no lanes. As we were driving back to the hotel, we all heard a loud "bang." Our bus hit someone. The bus driver said, "not to worry, this happens all the time and they're okay." That was an interesting welcome to Cairo.

April 1st, 2022—Sharm El Sheik and Mount Sinai, Egypt

I'm having breakfast at the hotel with a view of the beach hearing the waves smoothly landing on the desert brown sand and a colorful sunny sky. After getting up three times to refill my plate at the buffet, the chef was watching me in silence with what felt like a deep, disapproving look. I felt judged—as if the food he was serving on my plate was costing him personally. I was eating as much as possible before heading to Mount Sinai; it was going to be a long hike.

Also, I checked my bank account, and it was not pretty. I began to skip meals to save money. I consider myself a pretty generous person, never stingy but this was an expensive trip and I was currently working part time at Yoga Joynt trying to make ends meet while I was building my own podcast, The Awakened Journalist.

During breakfast, several birds came to visit my table. I was enjoying my book and paused to ask the birds telepathically if they had any messages for me. They said that tonight on the mountain, *Tita Marina*, my grandmother, my *Uncle Raúl*, and my cousin *Camilo*, who had all transcended, would accompany me on the hike to the cave where Moses received the ten commandments.

I kept reading my book, *Wisdom Codes* by Greg Baden. And as everything in the universe is synchronized, the chapter spoke about love and forgiveness as the forces that move your life. We are all born as love. *"Our challenge in life is to find within us everything that is not love."* Ancient Gnostic texts, discovered in the Nag Hammadi library, suggest that our vulnerability to pain is the gift and magical doorway to healing and to life itself. And I have proven it and experienced it by sitting with my pain and embracing it.

I get goosebumps every time I feel signs. The little hairs on my arms continued in eternal shivers on this trip. My friend Christine calls them "truth shivers." I went into the ocean before heading out, feeling my soul being purified with each dive into the majestic sea. A deep blue sea, an ocean of a thousand colors—abundant, healing and fully alive water. I shed subtle tears throughout the day, recharging my whole being with the light surrounding me from the celestial sun and this magical paradise.

The van picked me up at the hotel at 2:00 a.m. I barely slept and I was feeling anxious and excited to explore this sacred land. The ride was about two hours and I was asleep and awake all at once. I looked up at the sky on our drive and the stars were glittering all across the heavens smiling back at me.

When I got 750 steps from reaching the summit, my legs felt tired. I was eager to keep going and my legs weren't going to give up on me. Stopping more frequently to catch my breath, with each step, I tried inhaling vital energy, strength, bravery, and the will to go on as I was being very intentional with my thoughts. I felt my body recharging with my breath and the fresh oxygen from the mountain. Before the summit, we stopped at another little shelter where they offered us blankets for rent at 50 Egyptian pounds. Inside the hut, I already have two jackets on and still felt cold (I can't imagine what it's like at the summit out in the open air). The hut was filled with wool blankets and woven rugs from the time of my grandparents. They were clearly dusty and my allergies were acting up probably because they have never been washed. My fellow travelers had closed their eyes to rest before setting out again and so did I.

I woke up to the call at 5 a.m. to continue, feeling extremely tired. The temperature was in the mid-30s Fahrenheit, and I could feel my breath's warmth. It's said that we are the mountain, and those who hear the sacred call of these majestic beings, climb the mountains to know their heart. I truly felt that after all of my suffering and pain.

All tests to get here had been passed to the best of my ability in each present moment. I went into the cave where Moses received the Ten Commandments witnessing the Grand Rising of the father sun.

Tears sat on my eyelids, as I shed layers of past versions of myself that had served their purpose. I deserved to experience heaven on earth. I began to feel worthy of being loved again, vulnerably and transparently even those parts of myself I had found difficult to love. I felt my self-hatred leaving my body with every tear. I took a deep breath and felt the embrace of the mountain whispering: "all is forgiven; you're worthy of unconditional love."

Emiliana Molina Fajardo

Emiliana Molina Fajardo is a two-time Emmy Award Nominee and the founder of the podcast The Awakened Journalist (TAJ), where she does conscious journalism for the good of humankind. Her podcast was recently recommended by NBC-U-Academy as a beneficial resource for journalists and mental health.

Emiliana was honored with a White House Correspondents Scholarship in 2016 for her background in politics reporting and she has been named a "Global Changemaker" by the organization Global Changemakers for her podcast series Media Healers where she addresses mental health in the news industry.

She's a former White House News Correspondent, an excellence-driven and heart-centered transformational leader guiding you to embody and voice your heart's freedom of expression, authenticity and truth. She's also a certified angelic healer.

Connect with Emiliana on Instagram at @emilianamolinafajardo on YouTube and Spotify as The Awakened Journalist.

CHAPTER 9

Do I Lead from Hurt or Love?

Ingeborg Mooiweer

---

*I want to dedicate this chapter to all the women who
suffered from a toxic childhood and many lifechanging
experiences but somehow were able to find that little fire
within themselves to keep going and came out
on the other side as a phoenix.*

Once upon a time, there was a woman named Ingeborg, who had mastered the art of survival. Her life lessons had carved deep, invisible marks that only she could feel. In her peaceful village, time seemed to move slowly, but for Ingeborg, the world raced forward, always just out of reach. She constantly struggled to keep up, fighting day after day to stay afloat and stay ahead, even as life kept pushing her back.

This is her story.

It was one of those chilly autumn mornings, you know? I was sitting at my kitchen table, and despite the sunlight trying to sneak in, the cold just wouldn't budge — it clung to everything. My fingers wrapped around a black coffee mug; the warmth unnoticed. For a long time, I had stopped looking back; nostalgia felt like quicksand, ready to pull me under if I got too close. As I stared at the patterns in my coffee, my mind went meandering through the troubled and chaotic years.

My thoughts took me back to my early years, the origins of all that accompanied in later life. I lived in a big, old house that seemed packed to its rafters with secret shadows. My mother was the sort of woman whom one appreciated from afar, stunning and beguiling, in a way that others just wanted to accommodate. From a distance, she was perfect, except, right up close — she cracked like an old ornate mask worn at its edges. The air in the house would be tinged with my mother's heavy perfume. The scent was overpowering, when it should have been gentle, like raindrops simmering on pavement — a cover-up, trying to mask something darker lurking underneath.

There it was again: my mother's voice, like a cracked bell that would not stop ringing in my head as sharp and clear as the snap of a whip. There was always an unspoken expectation, a royal whisper for perfection. I had learned to be silent as a child; I was not allowed to show how I felt. My mother was hardly ever lavish with her praise, yet she was lavish with her remarks: "You are fat, stupid, and ugly." My mother could burst into anger over the smallest things — a speck of dust left behind, a wrinkle on a freshly ironed shirt, and would say in a chilling and narrow-minded tone: "There's only one kind of clean — the kind that leaves no trace, no flaw, no room for doubt. Anything less is a reminder that you're not enough." I felt like Cinderella and was scared.

I did my best always, but no matter how hard I tried, in the eyes of my mother there was just something about me. And by the time I was a teen, my mother's hopelessness for my success had moved in with me; it lodged on top of me, making it hard to breathe. I was already too used to hindsight, judging myself incorrectly for future historical mistakes. My mother's voice was the one in my head. I heard it constantly, never stopping, repeating how I would be nothing and that no matter what I did it wouldn't be good enough. The same old refrain echoed endlessly: "You can't do anything, hear anything, know anything, see anything." Over and over....

The lessons learned under that roof were hard ones — lessons in silence and self-denial, in the art of becoming small enough to fit into the mold my mother had crafted for me. Yet there was also something else beneath the surface, a strength that came not from defiance but from endurance. I had survived my mother's scathing remarks, her impossible expectations. I had learned to be the good girl, to anticipate my mother's criticisms before they were voiced. But there, too, lay the roots of something that would grow unchecked for years — a deep-seated belief that no matter how hard I tried, I would never be enough. It had taken root in the quiet spaces between my mother's words, in the silence that filled the house when I was alone and followed me even as I left that place behind.

I moved out as soon as I turned 16, determined to create some distance between me and my mother. I wanted to breathe air that did not smell of perfume and judgment; I longed for freedom. And as I settled into my first student apartment, and stuffed the tiny room with garage sale furniture, life wasn't what I hoped it would be.

Fast forward some years and my life took a deep dive into madness. I found myself in a hospital, battered and bruised with legs that would not move. The doctor spoke in his calm, assured voice, "You have an unknown disease that might never return you to the ability to walk." The words sunk in, causing a gaping feeling to expand within my chest, as if being slowly dragged into nothingness.

That year flew by in a haze of agony and anger. I learned how to negotiate life from a wheelchair. The most minor of actions, reaching for a glass from the top shelf or shifting my body in and out of bed, became wars I waged every day. The chair was now my world; I felt caged and stripped of all my independence. It had not only been a loss of movement, but was also an identity change. Who was I if not Ingeborg, who could run, and stand up, and dance, as well as walk, without giving it a second thought?

Recovery was slow and painful. My physical therapy sessions were a mix of agony and minor victories — moments when I might raise my leg an inch higher or balance for a few seconds more. The journey was bitter and sweet; I tasted failure and determination in equal parts. Every milestone, no matter how small, became a victory that kept me going. I dove into the exercises with the same determination I'd developed under my mother's watchful gaze, only this time it was for myself.

As I began to regain stability, my life started to look brighter. I was married with two kids, and another shock hit. His words were sweet, his promises bright, and I, so desperate yet oh so hopeful, placed my trust in him. I all but made him promise me, his words ringing in my ears, "That there would be a money back guarantee, you will have more than enough, no issues."

Finally, it was starting to look up, for a bit. The truth, as I later discovered, was that he was a grifter, and my money went up in smoke, leaving me with only the hollow echo of his empty promises.

I was consumed by the foul taste of betrayal. Everything I had been through, how careful and guarded I had been since that horrific time …

and still he fooled me. For weeks, I alternated between being angry at the man who had tricked me and furious with myself for falling for it. Many times, I thought — maybe my mother was right after all.

And then, just when life had given me all that I thought it could — as if the universe was not testing me enough — 2023 arrived and would tax me even more.

It all began in June. "Do you want to see your mother before it's too late?" asked my mother's friend. She had a stroke and was in the hospital. I hadn't seen my mother in 17 years, yet I felt the pull to go and seek closure. I took my kids with me, hoping to show her that I had done well in life despite the years apart. Our bond was never perfect, to say the least; we had always been at odds. She passed away two weeks later.

Later, as I walked into my mother's house to sort through things, the familiar scent of perfume hit my nose. It reminded me of my childhood when I knew my very presence could bring down wrath from above. The silence of her house nearly suffocated me, but I could almost hear my mother talking as I moved from room to room. It had always been there, hadn't it? A menacing ghost that even in death I could not escape.

Among my mother's belongings, it felt as if I was reading the years of history we had accumulated together. Boxes of old photographs, letters, and trinkets that once had so much meaning but now found their resting place on the table. This was the first time that I allowed myself to think of my mother not just as a figure of authority, but also as a human with fears and insecurities. Letters my mother had written but never mailed, napkins on which she scrawled things she was too haughty to utter. Alone now in the house I began to forgive, not just my mother but also myself.

Before grief could settle into my being, yet another bomb dropped.

While walking the Camino pilgrimage with my friend in July, I received a phone call that I never wanted to get. As soon as I heard my son's voice on the other end of the line, a sudden pressure squeezed into my chest as he informed me of my ex-husband's sudden death. My marriage had ceased to exist legally years ago, but the bond between us didn't just dissolve with the divorce papers. In that moment, it all came back to me, our life, memories of the old house, arguments over money, the way he would make me laugh until I could barely breathe. The grief touched my heart in a way I had not prepared for. It was as if an old wound came alive after decades of healing. The deepest ache I felt was for my kids, as their father was taken from them in an instant, gone forever. That split second shattered their world, and mine.

As I started to retread the road to recovery, summer brought another blow — the loss of my sister-in-law, my brother's wife, someone I had known for 30 years. Gone forever.

It almost felt mysterious. My mother gone, my brother lost his wife, and I had lost my ex-husband, all within three months. Could there be a lesson here?

The summer unfolded as a relentless storm, each loss carving new scars into my heart. Grief blurred the edges of my days, making the world feel unrecognizable. Yet, amidst the mourning, life demanded my attention in other ways. As I tried to rebuild some sense of normalcy, the unthinkable happened—what began as a season of loss transitioned into a season of fear.

The man I had been dating for over a year became someone I no longer recognized, his presence a shadow looming over my every move. Fear gripped me as I realized the man I had been dating for over a year had been watching me. Every sound sent chills down my spine. Each ring of the doorbell tightened the dread in my throat, turning my home into a place of terror.

One night, I spotted him — a shadow in the front garden, lit by the porch light. Panic surged as I called the police, my voice trembling. But when they arrived, there was no sign of a break-in, no evidence he had been there. Still, I knew what I had seen, and the fear hung heavily in the air. The police began checking on me regularly, but he didn't stop. Letters, emails, flowers — his obsession continued for a year until it culminated in a court case, which I won.

The memories that had seemed so heavy moments ago now felt lighter, as if by confronting them, I had stripped them of their power to hurt me. The years of enduring my mother's critical voice, of pushing myself to walk again, of fighting off the fear that came with being stalked, had each taught me to stand up for myself, to speak with my own voice, and to trust in my ability to overcome. Most importantly, they taught me to redefine what it meant to be strong. It wasn't about being unbreakable; it was about finding the courage to put the pieces back together, even when they did not fit perfectly.

I knew there would be more battles to face, but I also knew I would face them with the same resilience that had carried me this far. I am not just the sum of my hardships; I am a testament to the power of transformation, a reminder that even the most painful experiences can be turned into the very things that make us whole.

Once upon a time, there was a woman named Ingeborg, whose life was defined by a series of hard lessons, from a childhood steeped in tension to adulthood marked by loss and betrayal. As Ingeborg stood in her kitchen one brisk autumn morning, her hands wrapped around a steaming mug, she reflected on all that had happened to her and realized that while these events had shaped her, they did not define her. The process of overcoming these experiences had not only changed her on a personal level, but had also shaped her as a leader, teaching her lessons that she would carry forward to others.

Two things I learned:

Learning #1: Finding My Own Voice

Growing up with a narcissistic mother, I learned to keep the peace by anticipating others' needs, often at the cost of silencing my own voice. I sought validation from everyone but myself, until life's trials—the losses, the betrayal, the harassment—forced me to listen to my inner truth. This shift transformed me as a leader; I stopped prioritizing others' comfort over my convictions and began speaking up, even when it was unpopular. The change strengthened me and inspired my clients to be more authentic in their own lives.

My Tip for You: Journaling or meditation can be useful tools to gain clarity on what truly matters to you. When faced with a difficult decision, ask yourself, "What is my truth/feeling here?" Practicing small acts of assertiveness can help in building confidence over time.

Learning #2: The Power of Resilience

The year I spent in a wheelchair was one of the hardest tests of my resilience. Before, I had taken my physical abilities for granted, but afterward, every movement required effort and determination. I discovered that resilience isn't just about "bouncing back," but about adapting, adjusting, and finding new ways to thrive despite limitations.

As a leader, I learned to embrace setbacks as opportunities for growth. I encourage my clients to view failures not as dead ends, but as valuable learning experiences that could pave the way to innovation. I became more patient with others' mistakes, understanding that growth often comes through struggle.

My Tip for You: Build resilience by setting smaller goals, celebrating small wins, and practicing gratitude to stay focused on what you can control.

What is it that you want out of your life? Go for it. You got this!

Ingeborg Mooiweer

Ingeborg Mooiweer is an international pioneer in transformation, whose journey from adversity to empowerment has shaped her mission to change lives worldwide. Raised in Holland amidst uncertainty and emotional turmoil, Ingeborg learned resilience from a young age, navigating a challenging environment marked by parental divorce and the psychological abuse of a narcissistic mother.

Departing from her tumultuous home life at 16, Ingeborg pursued education in Hotel Management BSc, later relocating to London where she flourished in the Luxury Hotel industry for eight years. Finding love and starting a family, she balanced motherhood with a successful corporate career, eventually realizing her true calling lay in healing others' innermost traumas and challenges.

Ingeborg Mooiweer is an extraordinary artist and a profound business, strategic lifestyle and personal relationship alchemist. Her remarkable ability to navigate the complexities of human connections goes beyond surface-level interactions. With a deep understanding of healing and coaching, Ingeborg guides individuals and organizations towards transformative experiences.

In the realm of business, Ingeborg's insights into relationship dynamics are invaluable. She delves into the underlying layers of professional interactions, addressing hidden barriers and fostering healing within teams. By creating a safe space for vulnerability and open communication, she cultivates an environment where trust flourishes, collaboration thrives, and individuals are empowered to reach their full potential.

Known for her innovative techniques and swift results, Ingeborg employs a blend of analytical and feminine approaches to facilitate deep transformation in her clients. Highly intuitive, she navigates psychological barriers to facilitate meaningful change, equipping individuals with practical steps to progress forward.

Ingeborg's groundbreaking work has earned her recognition as a leader in her field, poised to share her insights with a broader audience through a forthcoming TED talk and book. Now available for interviews and speaking engagements, she invites media platforms to explore her remarkable journey and transformative methodologies.

Connect with Ingeborg at www.metamindbreakthrough.com.

CHAPTER 10

When Your Fascination with Life After Death Leads Your Life Journey

Lili Udell Fiore

To my beloved daughter, Esther, who is doing a
phenomenal job on her own journey.

Writing about one's life is an interesting challenge that forces additional reflection and if you are spiritual like me, it causes one to think about the mystical world in addition to daily life. I am a certified death doula and dementia practitioner. I also work with people on caregiving, planning a good death, and grief. Most people hear these subjects and run full speed in the other direction. But I run towards them and have always done so.

Since I was very young, I felt God's presence in my daily life. I also have always been curious about death. My parents told me that when

I was four years old I asked a lot of questions about where Dr. Martin Luther King went after his body died. That curiosity about death and life after death has never left me. So many questions filled both my heart and my mind that I have spent my lifetime reading books and talking to people to try and answer.

In addition to our going to the Episcopal church on Sundays, I began to investigate to learn about the mystical things in life. It started with a friend's mom who offered to do my astrology chart when I was around 15. She looked at me and stated, "You think about death a lot, don't you?" I answered yes, but was stunned as I didn't talk about it with most people, and I certainly never mentioned it to her. She said she knew because of my chart. I found that fascinating. Just to clarify, I was never thinking about self-harm or anything like that. I was simply intrigued by what comes after we die and leave the earth.

My journey with death sadly included losing over 20 people from the age of 15 to 20. Young and old alike, tragic stories and natural death due to age all came into my life. It is very hard to understand and comprehend why so many people I cared for died. By the time I was 25, there were more; beloved high school teachers and other friends. Although I believed and truly felt they were all with God, it was still very hard to cope with that amount of loss. At one point in my 20s, I stopped going to funerals because it felt as if I was bringing all of the sorrow from the loss with me to each service. Choosing mental health over depression, I allowed myself to have the space needed to process death and visit with their families and write letters telling them of my favorite memories of their person.

Even though I had lots of friends and a wonderful family, I never quite felt like I "belonged" or that I was too sensitive. I didn't understand why I felt things so very deeply. As an adult, I now understand that I am a high-level empath, and this is a superpower if you understand how to manage this gift. Even though my dad was an empath, I don't think he realized it either. It is an amazing thing to be able to tune into and pick up on people's feelings and emotions.

I loved growing up in Vermont and feel like I had a wonderful childhood along with my sibling, and our loving parents. However, when I was 16 years old, our mom developed a blood disease, A-Plastic Anemia, and was given six months to live. At the same time, our father was diagnosed with glaucoma damage and was told he would lose his sight over the next number of months. I could not understand why both of our parents had to have such horrible things happen to them. What was the purpose? I wanted to understand better why bad things happened to good people!

Mom thankfully did not die from her anemia but was very ill for three years. Dad eventually lost his sight. Our dad was the head of the Spiritual Care department of the big hospital nearby. He was also an Episcopal priest and taught Clinical Pastoral Education which is required by many religions to become a minister or priest. This training allows you to learn how to deal with tragedy so you can successfully help people cope with the tragedies, illness and death that is a part of life without falling apart yourself.

When we are young, it feels obvious when our lives end up being more difficult or challenging than our neighbors or classmates. We have not yet matured enough to know that hard times come at various points in our lives without rhyme or reason. We continue on. Sometimes we try to understand the "why" and other times we bury the question along with our feelings surrounding whatever issue or incident is causing us to question "why me" or "why my family."

Growing up, we would learn of various circumstances of tragedies and heartbreak which added to my empathic journey of feeling so much. Our dad was amazing and firmly rooted in his faith which allowed him to be incredible as he was there for both patients, their families and staff when they were dealing with tragedy, illness and death. Dad and I talked a lot about life after death and would tell me some of the stories that he had observed or been told by many patients who were dying, or were brought back after dying. I was fascinated by it.

My college years were interesting as I went through a few phases trying to understand who I was. My car was run into by a drunk driver in a pickup truck and was totaled, I got 44 stitches in my head. Fortunately, as we were hit I happened to look at my friend, Mary, and that saved me from having my face break the window. I dropped out of school for a while and moved into an apartment downtown and got a job as the assistant manager of a nearby bridal store. Eventually I got bored and my dad encouraged me to go back to school, which I did. I felt incredibly blessed that I looked at Mary at the last minute instead of watching the truck come towards us ... YIKES!!

When I was in my mid-20s, my allergies developed into an anaphylactic reaction and for the next 25 years I had multiple run-ins with smelling cinnamon, mold, or cats, causing my airway to close. One time when I was eating a cookie that, unbeknownst to me, had ingredients that I'm highly allergic to, I actually started to leave my body. I was confused because the medicine had always worked quickly, and I didn't understand why it wasn't. I never got to the tunnel that people talk about, but I did rise above my body into a ball of energy. I have never felt so alive as I did when I was dying. Happily, the EMTs arrived and gave me more adrenalin and I went back into my body. It's now 35 years later and I still remember what it felt like to be energy and outside of my body. It was amazing and so profound.

The only big hurdle I had in my faith was surrounding our dad. In my late 20s, I became very angry at God. Why had he not created a miracle for my dad? He gave the healing to others that my dad did a laying on of hands service for… so I didn't understand why he would not heal my beloved dad's sight when he had devoted his life to God and to helping people. It took me years to understand on the deepest levels that there is no understanding of the horrible things that we witness in life or experience first-hand.

I came to believe that everyone is on their own journey in life, and we are all in different stages and places. I take the belief that most people are doing the best they can with what they have and the things that I have a hard time accepting or witnessing. I have taken to telling God that "I need his help to deal with whatever the situation is because it is above my pay grade!"

I have relied on God throughout my life to help me make decisions about everything. Sometimes I didn't listen, but I realized that the mistake and the wrong road I took was actually a lesson and part of my zig zag.

I enjoyed a number of different jobs from working in retail at a boutique to working in business operations and marketing at IBM for 20 years. Even though some of the different careers I tried were not for me, I still learned a lot from working there, including selling funeral insurance policies for a few months.

In my 40s, I became a long-distance caregiver for my beloved Aunt Esther who lived outside of Chicago. It was hard to learn how to be responsible for an adult and feel confident when many of the people I worked with had their own agendas. Eventually I also became involved in the care for both of my parents as my sibling lived a few states away. Between the three of them, the journey as a caregiver along with my sibling lasted 12 years when all three were no longer here. I felt broken after our mom died from the cumulative stress of dealing with the caregiving and end of life work needed for all three. I needed a fun job, so I became a part-time salesperson at Victoria's Secret. I loved working with the customers and being on my feet and active.

We decided to move to North Carolina and leave the cold weather and grey skies of Vermont for the warmer climate and blue skies after my second husband retired. I could not stay in Vermont because there were too many memories of my life having lived in the same county from age six to 53.

When we were settled, I tried to work at a few other jobs but found that I couldn't do it. I still had too much to heal in my heart. Eventually, I had thoughts of becoming an end-of-life doula, but wasn't sure if it would be too depressing. Two years later, I had two friends in different states tell me about the online program at the University of Vermont. Taking it as a clear sign from God, I enrolled and found where I belonged. I thought that I would only work locally and do nothing else. Not surprisingly, God had other plans. Once I finished my certification, I came to know that I was also supposed to teach people how to deal with death and dying so that they could learn and carry the knowledge forward to help other families and friends.

As usual, God had more in store for me. I thought I would write a basic set of instructions on caregiving, using the lessons I had learned from our journey with our family. I also included numerous medical and personal care tracking and information forms to help caregivers get organized. I thought I was done with these things, and they were completed. NOPE, I got the message that there was more to say, and 15 chapters, over 500 pages and a year-and-a-half later, my book was complete.

I hadn't realized in high school that I talked about death and dying as much as I did. A dear friend of mine told me after I finished my book and certification, "It was always weird how you were interested in death and life after death, but now it all makes sense." Her statement was such validation for me. It helped me realize that all the not fitting-in feelings, curiosity, and unwavering belief in God had all brought me to where I am now.

At 60 years young, I am now happier than I have ever been. I have been blessed with my daughter and many wonderful years with my two ex-husbands. Has it been easy or perfect? Of course it hasn't, but that does not stop me from appreciating all the good times and love that was present for so many years. I finally feel like I fit in and have truly found where I belong in my work on caregiving, dementia, planning a good death, and grief. I am blessed to have an incredibly solid faith and belief in life after death that has enabled me to be able to speak on these subjects as well as help people who are going through one or more of these journeys.

Ultimately, I ended up covering far more ground as my zig zag approach and circumstances let me learn so much more that I would have had my life not included so many challenges and personal struggles. So please, it is okay if you don't feel like you fit in! Create your own group of friends and believe in the idea that there is a greater purpose for everything even if you don't understand the "why" in the moment.

Ironically, while I was working on this chapter, I saw an Instagram post that showed two wooden tracks for marbles. One of the tracks was at a slight decline, and the second track had hills and valleys which are the zig zags I am speaking of. Curiously, the marble that had to go through the valleys and up the hills arrived before the marble that had a straight decline. So maybe they are not so bad after all!

Lili Udell Fiore

Lili Udell Fiore has spent her life caregiving for various members of her family and friends. To ensure that all the lessons learned during the care for her parents helps others, she wrote Lili's Caregiver's Guide to allow people to benefit from the mistakes she made as a caregiver. Her various jobs and career paths led her to giving talks and trainings on caregiving, dementia, planning for a good death, and grief. Lili lives in coastal North Carolina.

Connect with Lili at https://muchlovelili.com.

CHAPTER 11

Rest to Rise: From Burnout to Breakthrough — My Lessons in Personal Leadership

Lynn Wong

To my husband, Mike, for your unconditional love and support; to Jill, for your unwavering friendship; to Judy, for inspiring me to coach; to David and Rita for your encouragement to become a coach; to Rita, for encouraging my sabbatical; and to Laura, for asking the life-changing question. Each of you has shaped this journey in ways words cannot fully capture.

The Leader I Was

It should have been just another Monday morning, but it was different. I just could not get out of bed. The weight of sheer fatigue created an invisible layer over my comforter and held me down. I had never ever felt this way before. There was no fever, no sore throat, no cold chills…just indescribable exhaustion that rendered me immovable. As soon as I acknowledged I was not going to work that day, another sense of knowing arose within me — this was the beginning of the end. I had not taken the break I needed so the break had come for me.

I somehow got around the fog of that morning to email my team that I was not going to be at work that day. I scanned my calendar and decided to keep just one afternoon meeting with my mentor. I found a late appointment that same day to see my doctor and crawled back to bed.

The afternoon meeting with my mentor was a gentle blur. I recall sharing how I was feeling horrible, yet without fever or any typical symptoms of the flu, or even COVID-19. I found myself apologizing profusely for my untimely crash. My mentor was kind and firm — he asked me to take the week off to fully rest, and to reconnect with him the following week.

Relieved by his permission, I proceeded to cancel the travel plans I had made to attend a leadership meeting in New York. I was wrecked with guilt as I had never once in my life missed a leadership meeting. I have worked at the world's largest companies in global retail and shipping, so I thrive on pressure, high-performing teams, and multimillion dollar deliverables, and have never crashed like this. My body was clearly sending me a message instructing me to stay still. My doctor's visit resulted in blood tests and referrals to other doctors for tests as well as my first doctor's note ever (as a professional) to take a week away from work to simply do nothing and rest.

The week that unfolded was intense. I remember sleeping a lot. I remember the relief when the doctor confirmed that my blood work did not reveal anything breaking or failing and to simply add 5000 IUs of Vitamin D to my daily supplement of Omega-6. She reminded me we were still waiting for results from my gynecologist and dermatologist for further evaluation.

I remember flashing back four months to my first bout with COVID-19. It was the sickest I had ever been — ten whole days of home quarantine and coughing my lungs out in the first four days. Amid the intense misery, I recall thinking to myself that I am grateful for the vaccine which should keep me from dying, but the unbearable, unstoppable hacking and wheezing inexplicably brought forth these questions, "Why am I still here? Why did COVID-19 take people who have more family and significance than I do?"

The dermatologist was able to see me by the end of the week. He confirmed that I had alopecia areata, an autoimmune condition that causes patchy hair loss, and that steroid injections could help me jumpstart recovery. Autoimmunity happens when our immune system gets confused and attacks tissues in our body, mistakenly assuming that they are foreign. Autoimmune conditions cannot be cured but can be reversed with lifestyle adjustments that prioritize one's well-being. Somehow, I had gone from being a hair donor to supporting the creation of wigs for cancer patients to almost needing a wig myself! I proceeded to take 12 injections to the bald spot about the size of my fist on the right side of my scalp. Maybe it was the 12 needles to my (presumably thick) head, maybe it was the result of surrendering to rest in the past week, maybe it was simply time for a serious lifestyle reset. I returned to work the following week and after a long discussion with my mentor, resigned from my job with one goal and no plan — to simply and actively rest.

This was not the way I had envisioned graduation from corporate life at all. This exit looked nothing like the cake and team celebrations that I had imagined at the retirement of a successful executive, decades later in life.

The Leader at Rest

I remember the night before I resigned. The last social media scroll that caught my attention before I set my smartphone down for the night was a question, "What would you do if you had six months to live?" A voice within me answered without hesitation, "Not this." That prompted me to check my bank account for the umpteenth time that week. The numbers confirmed I could afford to take six months away from work. That same voice piped up, "You cannot afford not to."

It was a tempting possibility to request unpaid leave from the company I worked for so I could have some level of job security to return to after a career sabbatical. Yet there was an inner knowing that I would not be able to fully rest if I did so. It was all indescribably scary yet freeing at the same time, trusting that I was the only one who needed to give me permission, and then simply surrender to rest, and allow life to unfold. It was time to begin my journey in personal leadership.

I had arrived in my life, to that moment described in pre-flight safety announcements about sudden changes in cabin pressure, to place the oxygen mask over my own face first before helping anyone else with theirs, even if they are family. During the first week of rest and the subsequent month before my last day at work, I had started to gain clarity about the three investments I would make to return to my health and well-being. I would commit to learn more about holistic health, get on the yoga mat, and join a global community of women working toward expanding their power, impact, and effectiveness as a human committed to a transformed world, rejecting the myths of scarcity, that more is better, and that things cannot change.

I invested the first 60 days resting in silence. Beyond my husband and two cats, there was very little I said to anyone in my life, online and offline. I slept a lot as well as followed up on the various doctors' appointments that ensued since my crash. A dense mass was discovered in my breast as well as a fibroid in my uterus. For someone who has always had a clean bill of health, with no allergies, no medication, no surgeries, etc., it was all enough to finally startle me into appreciating the decision I had made to reclaim my well-being. Taking a career sabbatical to prioritize self-care by learning more about how to meet and take care of me, with honesty and integrity from the inside out was the best decision I could have made.

The silence within the first 60 days of sabbatical was both healing and horrifying. There were so many days I would wake up to crashing waves of shame, fear, and guilt for cutting off my significant income flow and therefore shirking my financial responsibilities to contribute to my family's well-being. I berated myself for failing to live up to the potential others saw in me and wondered what I did wrong to deserve this fall.

I will always be grateful for the unconditional support of my husband, Mike, as well as my girlfriend, Jill, who were unwavering in their encouragement to be on this powerful pause in my life. My Mastermind group of Clifton Strengths-based coaches provided camaraderie and continuity as I moved from one phase of work to another. It helped to start holistic health education as well as regular yoga practice within days of completing my season of corporate life.

It was an unexpected reunion with a former sponsor in my corporate life that nudged me out of the solitude phase of sabbatical. We caught up over healthy smoothies one beautiful late summer morning at a local café. It was wonderful to reminisce how we met and so special to recognize we were both investing in powerful pauses to do the work of self-care and prioritize time with loved ones, both of which were impossible with the punishing pace of our corporate lives. She asked me a fateful question that shifted everything and all of me into my new season of work life integrity. She asked, "What are you going to do on the other side sabbatical, after you have rested?"

I was not expecting that question. My inner voice piped up, cautiously but clearly saying "I think I'm going to answer the call to coach." I loved global corporate work with large teams, but Coaching was calling for me to master my energy to help humans align to all that makes them come alive, to meet, and live their full potential. I loved winning on business teams and the higher up I moved in leadership ranks, the more success came from consistently prioritizing the development of my teams and mentees. I had already begun to invest in upskilling to become a coach after my expected retirement from corporate life. Yet I realized in that moment that I no longer had a rational excuse not to step up to do the work I love, starting now, to bridge people with possibilities, for themselves and others. Her response was immediate and surprising, "Now I know why I had a feeling I had to see you today...the local University is recruiting career coaches for their Executive MBA program. Please just have a conversation with them to explore."

She went on to introduce me with a glowing recommendation which led to interviews, and my official application. The next months also included the completion of my health and wellness coaching certification as I dove into the work of building my private, executive well-being coaching practice. My whole health continued to steadily improve as I dared to lean into the rest and prepare for a new, unexpected yet familiar season of professional work ahead. It was as if that fateful conversation had unlocked the path answering those life questions that surged during my hardest days with COVID-19.

The Leader Rising

I graduated from my career sabbatical into my bravest and best work to date. I learned so much during those months of purposeful rest and regeneration, in silence, and in generous community with diverse professionals. It was slowing down to be fully present with my whole being that created the space for me to re-learn self-care, release impostor syndrome, and realize I am the one I have been waiting for. I am the one to make choices that allow for my well-being and doing my best work. Taking full ownership of my career and well-being also meant releasing any remaining victim mindset that lingered. I learned and implemented the power of forgiveness of myself and surrendering to my strengths — applying energy to easeful work that creates value for myself and others. I learned that being healthy was so much more than a body without disease, that one's well-being includes honoring the interconnectedness of the mental, emotional and spiritual with the physical. I also learned that a life without dis-ease is simply, a life with ease.

In the training to become a health and wellness coach, we were regularly reminded we must be our first client before we can be of service to our clients. That was more than a practical recommendation – it was about being with integrity with ourselves, always. That reminder, along with the lessons to appreciate each human's multi-dimensional make-up (body, spirit, heart, and mind), unique health history, and evolution continue to inform my renewed well-being — as well as my work as an executive well-being coach to extraordinary global leaders in their season of transition and rediscovery of what it means to be well.

Much of my success at the world's largest companies was because I was the beneficiary of caring mentors, coaches, and sponsors. The powerful pause I invested in helped me discover my inner healer, meet my inner icon, and gain energy to do the work I love — guiding humans to meet and live their whole potential, in service of themselves and others.

This season of work life integrity where I am practicing daily what I guide my clients to do is not without its challenges and complexities. The work to release judgment, manage impatience and detach from controlling everything is hard. I meet my frustrations regularly with deep breaths, gratitude lists, and choices to believe everything happens for my benefit, even when those advantages are still unclear. Slow mindful stretches and impromptu one-song solo dance parties also help. I now take regular powerful pauses and participate in generous communities of inspired leaders to sustainably be and do my best work. My rest to rise career sabbatical has been a necessary path to embrace my whole self and come into alignment with all that makes me come alive so that I live out my full potential and help others along the way.

Answering my call to coach has been a journey of discovering the power of love at work and witnessing its positive ripple effects on our shared humanity. Upon becoming a certified International Health Coach, the always curious and occasional overachiever in me was also drawn to trauma-informed vinyasa yoga teacher training as well as becoming a National Board Certified Health and Wellness coach. The curriculum and communities of practice have helped me grow my personal and professional leadership in profound ways. Having the lived experience of leading inspired teams with the giants of industry and now getting to hone my skills of helping humans achieve their unique well-being is soul-satisfying and mentally expansive work.

It has been so fulfilling to get to guide and witness the transformation of my clients as they integrate their human doing and human being to discover a wholeness that is their unique well-being. I get to guide clients to embrace the simple definition of work as the creation of value for oneself and others, the secret to life as an acronym for "love in full expression" and integrity as a concept of wholeness with honesty. Several clients have reconnected with creativity and purpose after years of relentless professional demands from others. Others have made peace with past missteps and reframed them into growth opportunities. All have been able to revive important relationships and build new connections, personally and professionally. A client recently shared, "You provide non-judgmental accountability," and inspired me to pause with extra gratitude for the self-care, self-love, and lifelong learning practices that I now have and get to share in support of others.

I believe that a healthy, happy, regenerative world begins with healthy, happy servant leaders setting the standard and leading by example. I believe servant leaders who prioritize their well-being have the vital capacity, compassion and integrity to lead their families, teams, stakeholders and communities to create greater impact, with positive regard for the interconnectedness of all life. I am committed to guiding driven, accomplished leaders as they rest to rise, to gain energy and do the work they love, with and for the people that matter, with sustainable ease and excellence.

I meet my clients where they are in their season of life, inviting them into a virtual, bespoke incubator experience to move from exhausted to energized, guilty to grateful, feeling like an imposter to inspired as they navigate friction and flow to craft their next chapter with clarity and courage as they rest to rise. If you are curious about whether you are burning out or breaking through, or simply ready to explore a power pause in your life, I would love to hear from you.

Lynn Wong

Lynn Wong is a trailblazing executive well-being coach and career strategist who connects individuals with transformative opportunities. She co-creates with clients from various industries, including startups and Fortune 1-500 companies, to help them discover their unique work-life integrity compass to inspire meaningful work through personal challenges, professional growth and career sabbaticals.

Lynn's background includes leadership roles in international supply chain management at Maersk, Home Depot, Walmart and the New York Shipping Exchange. She holds multiple credentials, including National Board-Certified Health & Wellness Coach (NBC-HWC), Certified International Health Coach (CIHC), Certified Integrative Nutrition Health Coach (INHC), Certified Global Clifton Strengths Coach, Builder Profile Coach, and RYT-200 Trauma-Informed Vinyasa Yoga Teacher.

Originally from Singapore, Lynn also resides in the U.S. with her husband and their cats. Her career and passions have taken her across Singapore, China, and the U.S., and she is dedicated to visiting as many countries as possible. With an adventurous commitment to lifelong learning and exploration, Lynn's global experiences enrich her service as an EMBA Career Coach at the Sam M. Walton College of Business at the University of Arkansas and as a Board Member for the Community Clinic of Northwest Arkansas. Recognized as a member of The Outstanding Young People of Atlanta (Georgia) Class of 2008, she continues to inspire others through her love for food, travel, and discovery.

Connect with Lynn at www.lwcoaches.com.

CHAPTER 12

Power from Perseverance: Embracing the Rise

Melanie Marcia Morris

---

*To my father, who taught me resilience; to my husband
and partner, who showed me the power of love and
vulnerability; and to my children, who inspire me daily to
lead with authenticity and courage—this chapter is for you,
with all my heart.*

Growing up in San Jose in the 1970s and 80s was like living in a
kaleidoscope of change, innovation, and diversity. My neighborhood
was an intricate mix of black, white, and brown faces, a reflection of
what adults termed as a "melting pot" that the Bay Area was becoming.

As a mixed-race child—a blend of Black, White, and a bit of Latinx
heritage—this diversity should have felt comforting. Instead, it often

felt like I didn't fully belong anywhere. At school, I was "half-black-half-white," before the phrase "mixed race" was coined. At home, I was the daughter of a single Black father, living in a world where racial identities were rarely seen in such multiplicity.

Yet, our lives stood out in other ways. My father was a success story—a Black man thriving in real estate during a time when many doors remained closed to people who looked like him. He owned five real estate franchise offices, nearly two dozen rental properties, and the kind of material success that turned heads: a big house, multiple cars, and a boat that glided across the water like a proclamation of achievement. My father's success and our place in Silicon Valley's tapestry gave me hope that boundaries could be broken. But beneath the surface, my world was complicated. While I found ways to adapt and make friends, I was privately very lonely—scared to make real connections for fear of attachment and the potential to repeat the experience of a devasting loss.

Life moved forward as my surroundings demonstrated so clearly. Silicon Valley was in the infancy of its boom. It was exciting to be in the middle of it, and it provided a good distraction. The Bay Area's spirit of innovation and possibility planted a seed in me—a belief that I could embrace my differences, even if I didn't yet know how. I was a girl caught between cultures, grief, and the yearning to understand myself. This yearning would follow me through life, shaping how I face challenges, embrace triumphs, and learn the most profound lessons in perseverance.

A Childhood Shaped by Tragedy

Life's greatest lessons often arrive disguised as heartbreak, and mine came early. My earliest memory is one I commonly wish never happened. At just 5 1/2 years old, my life was shattered by a fatal car crash.

One moment, I was a little girl playing with my stuffed tiger in the back seat of my mom's car. The next, I was in a stranger's arms, being pulled from the wreckage of our vehicle, watching as paramedics attempted to save my unresponsive mother.

She was only 24 years old—just a month shy of her 25th birthday. I instinctively knew she was gone before anyone told me. When a nurse at the hospital gently confirmed my worse fears, my world as I knew it ended.

Back then, grief wasn't something you spoke about openly, especially to children. My father's doctor advised him not to talk about my mom's death, believing that I'd bounce back faster if we simply moved on. So, we tried. My mother's name was rarely mentioned, her absence was quietly acknowledged but never truly processed. By example, I learned to compartmentalize my emotions, to pretend the pain didn't exist.

This coping mechanism became my survival strategy. I buried my grief under layers of hard work, optimism, and a determination to build a "perfect" life. For years, it worked. Friends and family saw me as bubbly and resilient, and I basked in their admiration as a strong, resilient young lady. But deep down, I was unknowingly building a wall around my heart—one that would make future losses seemingly impossible to navigate.

Finding Belonging

At age 18, I met my first true love, Tim, the man who would become my husband, the father of our two sons, and the first person I believed could truly see me. He had grit and a steady determination that matched my own. For the first time, I felt safe enough to let someone into the parts of me I kept hidden.

Tim and I were young when we married—just 23 years old. We were kids ourselves when we started our family, welcoming our two sons in our late-twenties. Life with Tim was joyful and full of energy. We didn't have all the answers, but we tackled challenges as a team, believing that together we could achieve anything.

And for a while, we did. We achieved and lived what felt pretty perfect.

Tim became my rock, the anchor that kept me steady. I leaned into the life we built together, grateful for the partnership we shared. But life, as I would learn, has a way of testing even the strongest foundations.

When the World Shatters Again

Tim's death at 42 was sudden and devastating. Acute pancreatitis—a condition that came out of nowhere—took him from us in what felt like the blink of an eye. In an instant, the life we'd built together crumbled, leaving me alone to raise our teenage sons and navigate grief I wasn't equipped to face. I grew up as an only child with no mother. I had no template and very little frame of reference. I found myself asking "How in the world could I possibly raise teenage boys and be their primary example, all while as their sole provider and only parent?"

Losing Tim thrust me back to the helplessness of that 5 1/2-year-old girl. I didn't know how to cope because I had never allowed myself to fully feel the pain of my mother's death. I tried to be strong for my boys, just as I had been taught. I pushed my emotions aside and focused on survival.

But this time, the old strategy failed me. Grief has a way of demanding to be felt, and when I tried to ignore it, it seeped into every corner of my life. I made choices that reflected my avoidance rather than my healing. I entered into unhealthy relationships, sought distractions in material things, and avoided the very emotions I needed to process.

The worst moments were the ones where grief became too overwhelming to ignore. In those moments, I shut down completely, retreating from work, from friends, from life itself. Shame over my vulnerability kept me isolated, and I convinced myself that I was failing—not just as a mother, but as a person.

What I didn't understand then was that my vulnerability wasn't a weakness. It was the key to my healing.

The Turning Point

Years later, I came across an Instagram video from a young influencer. In it, he said something that shook me: "We GET TO feel our feelings." At first, I dismissed the idea. I had spent a lifetime believing that emotions were something to stuff away and hide, not something to embrace. But the more I thought about it, the more I became curious to explore this approach to healing.

I had spent so much of my life running from pain, fearing that if I allowed myself to feel it, it would overcome me. What I didn't realize was that by suppressing my emotions, I was denying myself the opportunity to heal.

So, I decided to try something new. I permitted myself to feel. At first, it was terrifying. Allowing myself to sit with uncomfortable emotions felt like opening a door I'd worked so hard to keep shut. But as I leaned into the discomfort, I discovered something unexpected: the feelings didn't destroy me. They freed me.

I started small, confiding in trusted friends and family members about my struggles. I found a therapist who provided a safe space for me to unpack decades of suppressed grief and learn healthier ways to process my emotions. The process was hard and took time. At one point, I committed to two therapy sessions per week for five weeks, which is when I had my biggest breakthrough. I must have cried multiple times a day, every day of these five weeks. It was a sort of cleansing. With each week, my courage to experience the painful parts of my life grew. Slowly but surely, I began to heal.

Redefining Strength

One of the most profound lessons I've learned is that strength isn't about presenting an unbreakable exterior. True strength is about showing up as our authentic selves, even when that self feels raw and exposed. It's about embracing vulnerability and allowing others to see you—not just your triumphs, but your struggles too.

For years, I equated resilience with perfection. I believed that as long as I appeared strong, I was strong. But the truth is, resilience isn't about never falling. It's about rising after every fall, no matter how hard it is.

"The greatest glory in living lies not in never falling, but in rising every time we fall." ~Nelson Mandela

---

And rising doesn't mean doing it alone. Some of the most significant moments of my healing have come from the connections I've built with others—friends, family, and even strangers who have shared their own stories of loss and perseverance. In those connections, I've found a sense of belonging and support that I never realized I needed.

The Glory in Rising

Looking back, I see that every challenge I've faced has taught me something valuable about myself and the world around me. Losing my mother taught me the importance of honoring grief rather than suppressing it. Losing Tim taught me that it's okay to lean on others when life feels unbearable. And learning to embrace my emotions has taught me that healing isn't linear—it's a journey filled with setbacks and breakthroughs.

The greatest glory in life isn't in never falling. It's in finding the courage to rise again, no matter how often life knocks us down. And each time we rise, we reclaim a part of ourselves that fear and resistance tried to steal.

Lessons from the Journey

If there's one thing my journey has taught me, it's this: life's triumphs often lie in the quiet moments of perseverance. They're not always the grand, fairytale victories we imagine. Sometimes, they're as simple as getting out of bed on a hard day, asking for help, or allowing ourselves moments to reflect.

If you feel overwhelmed by your own trials, know this: you are not alone. It's okay to feel your feelings. It's okay to ask for help. And when ready, it's okay to rise—not because you have to, but because you deserve to.

In rising, we find our strength. In rising, we discover our power. And in rising, we reclaim the glory that is uniquely our own.

Leading and Living with Purpose

The journey through my own trials, triumphs, and healing has shaped not just who I am, but why I lead. At the heart of my purpose lies a deep desire to empower others to embrace and express their authentic selves. For so long, I believed success came from masking pain and showing up as strong, but my journey taught me that our greatest power lies in leaning into our experiences—both joyful and challenging. When we connect meaningfully with others, we foster environments where people feel safe, valued, and capable of their best work and their fullest lives.

As a mother, this shift in perspective has profoundly impacted my relationship with my sons. They've seen me navigate grief, vulnerability, and growth, and I've been intentional about sharing my lessons with them. My hope is that by modeling authenticity and courage, I've given them the courage to face their own challenges and embrace their emotions as a source of strength rather than a weakness. Through this authenticity, our bond has deepened. I'm proud to share that I've seen them rise as empathetic and grounded young men—who would make their dad, Tim, beam with pride.

My approach to authentically feeling my feelings has also transformed my leadership. I've seen firsthand how empowered teams thrive when individuals feel free to bring their full selves to their work. By fostering an environment of authenticity, I've helped teams collaborate more meaningfully, innovate boldly, and overcome challenges together. The clarity and connection that come from leading with purpose and vulnerability have led to some of the most rewarding outcomes in my career.

Courage to Trust Again

Some years after Tim's passing, I was lucky to find love again—with my dear Patrick. Perhaps as important to my journey, embracing vulnerability has allowed me to connect more authentically with Patrick. Through honesty and vulnerability, I've learned to let go of the need to be "strong" all the time and to trust him with my fears and dreams. In turn, Patrick's unwavering support has been a reminder that love and partnership flourish when built on openness and shared humanity.

Together, we've created a space where both of us can thrive as our authentic selves, and that has been one of my greatest joys.

Finding love again with Patrick has shown me that true partnership isn't about perfection but about showing up fully, flaws and all. This newfound openness has brought joy, peace, and fulfillment I once thought impossible.

Melanie Morris

Melanie Morris is an accomplished organizational development (OD) leader and executive coach, boasting extensive expertise in leadership development and change management. Her dedication lies in nurturing inclusive and growth-centric organizational cultures. Melanie excels in crafting strategies that empower leaders and organizations to realize their visions and achieve their business goals.

Melanie has served as an executive coach and organizational development partner for a diverse array of industries and prominent companies from Fortune 500 companies, specializing in tech, pharma, and research industries. Notably, she is currently pursuing a Ph.D. in Global Leadership & Change, further enhancing her credentials in this field.

Connect with Melanie at https://bloomforward.com.

CHAPTER 13

Seek to Understand

Melanie B Schwarz

This chapter is dedicated to my family. Their support has
been unwavering as I have pursued
my dreams and passions.

Pulling the veil away from your leadership style is a vulnerable moment. You have to look deep inside, be self-reflective, honest, and tell people the "why" behind your characteristics and style. I have had the privilege of many years of experience, amazing mentors, truly dynamic training and education, and many canvases on which to practice. I learned that each leader is unique, and whether you are leading or following, there must be mutual respect and understanding. That is the key to sharing your "why." People don't have to agree with everything you do as long as they understand your foundation. Great leaders are able to take all of their experience and build it into a beautiful mosaic that they are proud to share with others. You, too, get to build your own truly unique leadership style. You will know you have nailed it when the people on your team walk alongside you on a healthy, respectful, and successful path. I encourage you to deeply consider your values, your core personality, and how you want others to feel next to you as a leader.

Here is the story of my "why" and four key lessons that have formed my leadership style and helped me to find MY deeply held values on which to build a foundation, one where others want to join me on the journey to purpose, success, and community building.

Lesson One: You Have to Get in the Arena

Lesson Two: Your Survival Matters

Lesson Three: Life is a River

Lesson Four: Build Your Leadership Story

Lesson One: You Have to Get in the Arena

You can't be a successful leader unless you get "in the arena." The words of Theodore Roosevelt from his famous speech "The Man in the Arena," nailed this concept. As you read each word decide if you are the critic or the man/woman daring greatly. Leaders dare greatly every day.

"It is not the critic who counts; not the man who points out how the strong man stumbles, or where the doer of deeds could have done them better. The credit belongs to the man who is actually in the arena, whose face is marred by dust and sweat and blood; who strives valiantly; who errs, who comes short again and again, because there is no effort

without error and shortcoming, but who does actually strive to do the deed; who knows great enthusiasms, the great devotions; who spends himself in a worthy cause; who at the best knows in the end the triumph of high achievement, and who at the worst, if he fails, at least fails while daring greatly, so that his place shall never be with those cold and timid souls who neither know victory nor defeat. " ~Theodore Roosevelt

---

Learning to get into the arena happened to me in a very unique way when I was asked to teach communications at our state women's prison. A job that nobody wanted and that I couldn't wait to try. I received extensive training from the many professionals who protected me. Still with every visit, I wasn't prepared for the environment or the fear. The fear was of the unknown. I had never been in a prison, nor had I spent much time with those who had committed a serious enough crime to have them behind bars. What I found was a large population of women from every walk of life living together bonded by the fact they had all been convicted of a felony.

The prison guard assigned to me was concerned that I would be easily manipulated. She wasn't wrong. I found myself many times overly emotional or becoming attached to their stories. I quickly learned to get a tougher skin, but I also realized that these women had never learned any other way to communicate or act. Their lives had been hard, and I had no frame of reference for where they came from.

Over the two years I was there, I did teach them communication skills, but they taught me to withhold judgment and spend time learning about their lives. Their stories and histories changed me for the better. I can only hope that everyone gets an experience like this, to be immersed in a culture that is not your comfort zone. This is where deep introspection and learning happens, and this is where core values are forged. I still volunteer with our local community corrections facility to continue my learning and explore ways to help those re-entering our communities in a safe and healthy way.

Lesson Two: Your Survival Matters

You may be asking why I had to take a job teaching in a prison. That fateful and life-changing opportunity came from a failure. After a very successful sales career, I decided I was ready to own my own business and take my skills and this experience into the world of marketing. Yes, I had the skills, but what I didn't have was the world experience of evaluating a new landscape where I owned every decision. I also did not realize the importance of vetting your partners. I trusted everyone, and it never occurred to me that someone would want to partner with me who didn't share my vision and values. Lesson learned, and bank-ruptcy followed.

The humiliation of being conned by a friend and the realization that I gave my life and family's well-being to a person who didn't have a moral compass crushed me. I withdrew and became incredibly withdrawn. What had I missed? I had been so enthralled by the idea of a successful business that I made horrible choices to get to what I thought was important. I had never experienced failure at this level and when you add this to your experience portfolio (baggage) trust me it stays with you forever.

To this day, I know not to chase the shiny penny, but to chase the people who are doing good work and have values similar to my own. Failure is hard, but rebounding, and not punishing yourself every day is harder. Be kind to yourself and make new and better choices with what you know now. Also, stay in the arena because it is the only place to make a true difference. Never let those on the sidelines deter you.

My other strong recommendation is to learn to withhold and release judgment. How people come to experiences can only be fully understood by them. It is not your job or place to make judgments of others. It is your job and place for YOU to decide whether you can empathically understand their circumstances and choices and if YOU want to engage. Although other's decisions and actions can be challenging, they can also have a very important role in your path and bring great diversity and understanding.

I learned to release judgment from my oldest daughter. She is the light of my life. She and her sister have brought me incredible joy. However, joy turned to challenge when we discovered she was suffering from a substance use disorder or addiction. Now my role was not as a leader but as a parent. My sole responsibility was her well-being and I thought that meant removing the disease from her life. For a ten-year period, I threw every resource I could find at her and her addiction. It came at the detriment of my other child, my marriage, my career, and mostly myself. I gave up everything to prove that I could beat this. What I realized, albeit slowly and painfully, was that it wasn't my battle to conquer. It wasn't my disease. During this time, I was labeled as an "enabler." A common term for those supporting or trying to control someone else's disease of addiction. The title was accurate but cruel, and I was determined to be a sounding board for others in the same situation.

I wrote a book about my personal experience in the hopes of sharing it with others in a similar experience. The book is called "*LifeJackets: A Mother's Journey Through Her Child's Addiction*." The takeaway is simple, you can't save someone from their own actions, you can only save yourself and find a way to live YOUR life. These 10 years were not only a personal journey, but they also educated me on my next career path and leadership tenet summed up nicely with this quote.

"One day you will tell your story of how you overcame what you went through and it will be someone else's survival guide." ~Brene Brown

---

Lesson Three: Life is a River

The metaphor of the river is strong in all of my work, and it resonates because the beauty of a river is it never stops until it gets to its final destination and even then, it continues to move. Each stage reflects the river's journey from its source to its destination, shaping landscapes, and supporting ecosystems along the way.

Rivers are also incredibly important for the livelihood of many species and plants that keep our world fresh and alive. Living in Montana, we are surrounded by natural beauty, and many, many rivers, and streams. They are our compass, and we know to respect their power, enjoy their recreation, and know they are headed to the next great river or ocean to complete their journey. This is a great way to live your life; always changing, fresh and alive, naturally beautiful, powerful, fun, and a true compass guiding your values.

Several years ago, in my small Montana city, we had an oil pipeline leak into our beautiful river. A significant spill. The response was overwhelming. People were angry about the spill and that it could even happen. They criticized the oil company. But what happened next was amazing. Every resource from around the country descended on our town to help with clean-up, manage the wildlife affected, inform the community about safety, and so much more. I watched the precise delivery of their crisis plan and how seamlessly they worked together to help the river recover. They had miscalculated upstream, but they had a plan for the "in case of emergency."

A few weeks later a colleague and I were talking about the response, and we commented, "What if this was our response for those who live in our city who are in crisis?" The homeless, those with mental health disorders, those living in poverty, those experiencing a substance use disorder, those involved in a domestic violence situation, and those who turn to crime to survive. AND what if, in addition to having a solid crisis plan, when situations or people fall through the cracks or into the river, we also had reliable and abundant safety nets upstream so that the numbers would be much smaller in a crisis. We agreed this model and dual approach would be most effective for people too. First, prevention, then comprehensive triage in an emergency. It taught me a strong lesson of planning and making the best decision you can at the moment, but to always be prepared for an emergency or crisis. Your team counts on you to be well-rounded, logical, and empathic, but mostly, ready for changing circumstances.

"There comes a point where we need to stop just pulling people out of the river. We need to go upstream and find out why they're falling in." ~Desmond Tutu

---

Every time I read this quote, I pause and ask myself, "Am I building a pipeline to enhance others' lives, or am I still stuck in the crisis management mode only triaging without real change?" You see, you can't create a new vision or go upstream if you spend all of your time only finding resources to help people out of the river. In fact, you can't even imagine a different experience because day after day you are problem-solving for others or managing crises for your organization.

You must spend time learning the changes that could be made upstream to improve people's outcomes.

One's personal journey will take the same path as many rivers. There will be calm and peaceful moments upstream, bathed in sunshine and happiness. There will be days of rain and flooding, overflowing your banks with overwhelm and anxiety. There will be rapids that toss you helplessly around, losing control of your bearings. There will be waterfalls that look calm going in only to dump you quickly downstream into an unknown abyss. And there will always be motion, movement, changes. Each circumstance, happy, sad, or earth shattering will be temporary. There will be a next phase, a new current, and an undeterred force pushing you to move on. Life is a river.

Lesson Four: Build Your Leadership Story

Now picture your river and the two points of impact. Upstream where you have the power and responsibility to make choices for yourself and others before they head downstream. OR living downstream where the outcomes are already decided for you, and you are forced to react based on limited resources and knowledge of how they got here. The truth is you will spend time in both locations, but as you grow as a leader you will find you get more opportunities upstream and this will define your purpose and how you decide to use your resources and influence for positive downstream results.

I realized I had spent much of my career finding and creating resources for those in a challenge or crisis when my real interests lay in keeping people from falling into the river. Thus, the development of my UpStream Leadership Strategy. I committed to spending equal time on both parts of this equation and I made a long-term plan to fully implement UpStream thinking into my world, both work and personal, every day.

All this to be summed up with my final and maybe favorite quote, from me. After a year-long leadership masterclass and a personal deep dive into how to fully execute an upstream philosophy, we were asked to write our personal leadership statement. Here is mine.

"Foster a culture of empathy, respect, and collaboration. Communicate graciously, listening with intention, and speaking with clarity. Open doors of opportunity for others, stewarding them towards their greatest dreams and potential." ~Melanie B. Schwarz

---

Now it is your turn. Write your leadership story and share it widely with others and invite them to join you on your journey.

Melanie Schwarz

Melanie Schwarz is the current CEO of UpStream Strategy Partners, a collaborative company designed to educate communities around mental health and substance use disorders in the workplace. She designed a curriculum for businesses titled Mind Wellness University. Mind Wellness University is a workplace membership designed to support employee mental health through online and in-person learning opportunities customized for the unique needs of each workplace.

Melanie previously worked as the Chief Growth and Innovation Officer at a regional substance use and mental health treatment center in Montana, and before that was the Director of Business Development for the local economic development organization.

Melanie is also an advocate for families amid their loved one's substance use disorder. Having lived this herself, Melanie is very familiar with the journey people are on and the need to try and navigate this disease from a support or parent role.

Melanie is a published author. Her book *"LifeJackets: A Mother's Journey Through Her Child's Addiction,"* has helped hundreds of families with their experience of substance use disorder in their family.

"*LifeJackets*" is Melanie's first book and has launched her dream of traveling the country and talking to other families experiencing addiction.

Melanie lives in Billings, Montana, and is married with three adult children. She has had a 25+ year career in marketing, public relations, and fundraising. She is a graduate of Montana State University.

Connect with Melanie at www.leadupstream.com.

CHAPTER 14

Intentional Growth Mindset

Precious Nyarambi

This is dedicated to all women desiring growth in all aspects of their lives and live a balanced life, remember to lift as you rise always.

A growth mindset is a belief that abilities, intelligence, and talents can be developed and improved over time through dedication, hard work, and learning. This concept, introduced by psychologist Carol Dweck, contrasts with a fixed mindset, where individuals believe their talents and intelligence are static and unchangeable. People with a growth mindset see challenges as opportunities for growth, view failure as a learning experience, and understand that effort leads to improvement and success.

Why a Growth Mindset Is Important

- Increases Resilience and Persistence.

- Encourages Lifelong Learning.

- Enhances Motivation and Performance.

- Improves Relationships and Collaboration.

- Boosts Innovation and Creativity.

In essence, a growth mindset fuels personal and professional development, making it essential for individuals and organizations aiming for continuous improvement, adaptability, and success in a dynamic world. A growth mindset, one that allows us to adapt, persevere, and seize opportunities, is fundamental to both personal and professional success. As people, we are designed to evolve, learn, and move beyond stagnation. Growth is often a product of desire, exposure, and the willingness to confront our own limitations. I realized that one of the main reasons my business struggled to grow was because I wasn't growing. My personal and emotional attachments to the organization became a barrier, hindering its progress. As I expanded my mental capacity, my business began to flourish.

One significant moment in my journey involved a mentor who tried to impart critical insights to me. While the advice was well-meaning, I was too emotionally tied to my business to fully grasp it at the time. I wasn't ready to receive that wisdom, and it took me time to understand and implement it. Only when my mind opened to new perspectives did I recognize the value of those lessons. It taught me that the business landscape is ever evolving, requiring a pragmatic approach to stay relevant. A growth mindset requires the mind to be continuously renewed, ready to embrace new insights.

There's a saying: "Write the vision and make it plain." For me, once you articulate your vision, the next step is to work backward, engaging in actions that support your ultimate goals. Success doesn't happen by accident; it requires hard work, perseverance, smart decisions, and, above all, passion. Aligning purpose, vision, and a growth mindset with the concept of "The Power of Yet" creates a path of continuous growth. As psychologist Carol S. Dweck explained, "not yet" transforms fixed mindsets into opportunities for learning. This simple word, "yet" brings confidence and encourages a different perspective, empowering us to see challenges as steppingstones toward achievement.

In the entrepreneurial journey, challenges are inevitable. Yet these difficulties are catalysts for growth, pushing us to refine our problem-solving abilities. Personally, I handle challenges by pausing to reflect, dissecting the issue, and working out a solution. Facing and overcoming each obstacle builds resilience. The more challenges we conquer, the more equipped we become for future hurdles. This cycle of challenge, reflection, and resolution builds a form of mastery, turning us into victors rather than victims. Entrepreneurs who embrace challenges grow in their capacity to see opportunities in every setback.

A growth mindset also fosters openness to learning, whether from criticism, the successes of others, or personal failures. Entrepreneurs recognize that every experience, even failure, contributes to a larger picture of growth. The mind is a powerful tool; filling it with positive thoughts and possibilities enables a life of flourishing. What we focus on in our minds often becomes our reality. With this approach, a growth mindset evolves from simply believing in potential to actively cultivating it. When combined with guidance and an open heart, the growth trajectory becomes a lifelong path of self-improvement and increased relevance.

Purpose, vision, and a growth mindset form the foundation of impactful entrepreneurship. Purpose fuels the persistence needed when profits aren't yet realized, and it drives us to pursue goals beyond financial gains. Purpose can bring about a deep sense of fulfillment that money alone cannot provide. A strong purpose often attracts resources, aligns opportunities, and creates the energy needed to overcome challenges. Starting is often the hardest part, but the momentum gained by just beginning builds toward greater accomplishments.

Imagine if everyone knew their purpose. The impact on communities and society would be transformative. When purpose is aligned with our skills and values, it leads to lasting contributions that extend far beyond individual achievements. Finding purpose doesn't always happen immediately, but it is something worth pursuing with resilience. If purpose feels elusive, "yet" can be a reminder to keep striving, knowing that clarity will come. Living with purpose not only alleviates loneliness by filling our lives with meaning, but it also provides a compass for making the most of our time.

Conviction and belief are key drivers of purpose. I believe that we are called to overcome and succeed, to act with purpose and resilience in the face of adversity. True conviction fuels a willingness to defy odds and a drive to stand by one's principles. It's this strength that allows us to rise above challenges and achieve against all odds. When one identifies their purpose, a journey of self-discovery begins that reveals the unique potential each of us carries. Purpose-driven individuals become torchbearers for others, demonstrating that overcoming obstacles is possible and inspiring others to do the same.

One of my favorite stories illustrating the power of purpose is that of Grameen Bank, which serves as an example of how addressing unmet needs can lead to groundbreaking ideas. Nobel laureate Muhammad Yunus founded Grameen Bank to provide affordable credit to impoverished women in rural Bangladesh, based on a deep understanding of their needs. His idea stemmed from thorough needs analysis, which revealed a significant gap in economic opportunities for these women. This insight allowed Yunus to create an institution that empowered countless women, transforming entire communities in the process.

The story of Grameen Bank resonates with me, as I too have encountered barriers due to a lack of funding or support. Like many, I have faced the difficulty of securing resources without collateral. Many viable projects remain on hold because traditional lenders prioritize collateral over potential. Yunus's innovative approach — peer-group lending — demonstrated that with the right model, financial inclusion is possible even for the marginalized. His commitment to meeting a real need despite resistance serves as a reminder that social entrepreneurship often involves challenging norms to achieve meaningful impact.

The balance between addressing community needs and recognizing community assets is vital. Some, like John McKnight of Northwestern University, argue that focusing too much on needs can paint communities as deficient. He advocates for "asset mapping," an approach that highlights the strengths within a community, from local businesses to health centers. When combined, need-based and asset-based approaches create a comprehensive view that fosters resilience and innovation.

Social enterprises play a unique role in addressing needs that traditional sectors often overlook. By meeting basic needs, connecting people to resources, and advocating for policy changes, social entrepreneurs bridge gaps and drive community resilience. The integration of needs and assets becomes a strategy for sustainable development. Yunus's journey exemplifies this — he understood the entrepreneurial potential of Bangladeshi village women and leveraged it to address their financial needs, laying the foundation for a lasting institution.

When venturing into new markets or starting initiatives, understanding both the challenges and assets within a community allows for sustainable solutions. Each community holds untapped resources that, when recognized and nurtured, become powerful catalysts for transformation. The work of Community Wealth Ventures (CWV), which helps nonprofits leverage their assets for income, exemplifies how rethinking resources can lead to innovative solutions. The key is to view challenges not as setbacks but as opportunities for creative problem-solving.

The trials and frustrations we encounter often contain the seeds of our greatest breakthroughs. Embracing challenges with a problem-solving mindset turns them into powerful learning experiences. Like Yunus, I have found that the obstacles I face fuel my motivation to seek solutions, not only for my benefit but for those around me. Each success story begins with overcoming challenges, transforming individuals into resilient problem-solvers who inspire others to do the same.

Purpose-driven entrepreneurs understand that the challenges they face are not solely for personal growth; they are steppingstones toward greater societal impact. Through trial and perseverance, we uncover the depth of our abilities and the resilience within. Social entrepreneurship requires a conviction to address real needs and pursue meaningful change. Purpose, once discovered, sustains us through difficult times and drives us to create solutions that have lasting benefits for our communities.

Moreover, purpose is intrinsically tied to impact. When we work in alignment with our purpose, we create ripple effects that positively influence others. As Yunus's example shows, pursuing a legitimate need can transform communities and inspire countless others. Purpose doesn't just bring personal fulfillment; it attracts resources, support, and partnerships that enable us to multiply our impact. We all have the potential to be catalysts for positive change, lighting the way for others through our dedication to purpose.

As social entrepreneurs, understanding the needs within our communities while recognizing their assets enables us to address complex issues effectively. Communities are rich with both needs and resources, and our work lies in bridging these elements to foster resilience. The challenges we face are not mere roadblocks; they are training grounds that develop our capacity to enact meaningful change. By adopting a growth mindset and cultivating purpose, we become part of a larger narrative of societal transformation.

To truly make a difference, we must embrace a collaborative approach, recognizing that our efforts are interconnected. Purpose-driven endeavors rarely succeed in isolation; they require the support and collaboration of others who share a similar vision. The combined efforts of individuals and organizations create a synergy that amplifies impact. When we pursue our purpose, we inspire others to do the same, creating a powerful network of change-makers.

The journey of purpose is not always straightforward. It requires resilience, adaptability, and a commitment to continuous learning. By cultivating a growth mindset, we open ourselves to new possibilities and prepare ourselves to navigate an ever-evolving world. Each obstacle becomes an opportunity for personal growth, and ultimately, for contributing to the greater good.

We are each part of a master plan. Our individual contributions shape the future and influence of those around us. Embracing purpose and pursuing it with conviction allows us to transcend personal goals and work toward collective transformation. By choosing to rise to our potential, we become agents of change, fostering resilience and hope in our communities. As we align our purpose with our actions, we build a legacy that empowers future generations to do the same.

Female entrepreneurs across the world, particularly in regions like Africa, are increasingly rising above the barriers they face by embracing a growth mindset infused with a strong sense of purpose. This powerful combination enables women to transcend challenges such as limited access to capital, societal norms, and family responsibilities. By seeing obstacles as opportunities for growth, learning, and improvement, women are turning adversity into triumph, not just for themselves but for their communities and even the global economy.

1. Shifting from Fixed to Growth-Oriented Thinking

A growth mindset encourages female entrepreneurs to shift from a fixed perspective, where challenges seem insurmountable, to one where obstacles are seen as opportunities to develop skills, build resilience, and learn from mistakes. Women are more willing to take risks and try innovative solutions to problems, instead of letting failures define their capabilities.

Purpose-driven women are more likely to approach their businesses with optimism, knowing that their entrepreneurial journey is about more than just financial success. Their purpose could be empowering other women, addressing societal issues, or improving their communities. This purpose fuels their desire to overcome obstacles.

2. Embracing Financial Barriers as Growth Opportunities

Financial barriers are among the most common challenges faced by female entrepreneurs. However, women with a growth mindset don't see financial limitations as something that will hold them back — they see it as an opportunity to think outside the box and innovate in finding solutions.

Purpose-driven women see financial independence to create more impact. They might face the challenge of raising funds but remain focused on their larger goals of making a positive difference in society. This resilience is a direct result of their ability to reframe financial struggles as a temporary hurdle to overcome, not a permanent roadblock.

3. Navigating Societal and Cultural Barriers

In many societies, traditional gender roles and cultural expectations limit women's opportunities in business. However, female entrepreneurs with a growth mindset understand that these societal norms do not define their potential. They embrace these challenges as opportunities to challenge and change the status quo.

Infused with a purpose to create economic and social change, these women often lead by example. They inspire others to break free from societal limitations, proving that women can be leaders, innovators, and successful business owners.

4. Overcoming the Challenges of Family Responsibilities

Balancing family responsibilities with entrepreneurship is a common barrier for female business owners. Traditional gender expectations often place a heavier burden on women to take care of household duties, which can limit their time and resources to focus on their businesses. However, a growth mindset helps female entrepreneurs approach this challenge with flexibility and creativity.

Women with a growth mindset are more likely to embrace adaptive strategies such as time management, outsourcing, and leveraging technology to streamline their business operations, creating more space for both their professional and personal lives. They may also redefine success by incorporating personal and family values into their business models.

With purpose at the core, female entrepreneurs are driven to create businesses that allow them to balance their personal and professional lives while pursuing their passions. They often build businesses that also create value for others, such as childcare services, flexible work environments, or health-focused initiatives.

5. Transforming Challenges into Strategic Business Opportunities

Challenges such as limited access to markets, resources, and information often hinder the growth of female-led businesses. However, female entrepreneurs with a growth mindset are not deterred. Instead, they take these barriers as an opportunity to innovate and become more resourceful.

Purpose drives them to identify untapped markets or create products that address specific needs in their communities. By leveraging creative solutions and strategic thinking, they find ways to scale their businesses without relying solely on traditional resources or networks.

6. Building Supportive Networks and Collaboration

Networking is vital for entrepreneurial success, but for many women, access to influential business networks may be limited due to cultural or gender barriers. Entrepreneurs with a growth mindset understand that building a network is a long-term process and take active steps to connect with mentors, peers, and partners.

With purpose at the center, women entrepreneurs are more likely to seek out networks that align with their mission, whether it's women-focused groups, social enterprises, or organizations that champion diversity and inclusion. They are also more likely to pay it forward by mentoring and supporting other women in business.

7. Harnessing Technology and Digital Platforms

Technology has become a game-changer for female entrepreneurs, allowing them to overcome geographic, financial, and logistical barriers.

Female entrepreneurs with a growth mindset are quick to adopt digital tools and online platforms to scale their businesses and reach global markets.

Infused with purpose, women use technology not just to grow their businesses but to create meaningful social change. Whether it's creating an online platform for education, leveraging e-commerce to sell handmade goods, or using social media to promote awareness on social issues, technology serves as a vehicle for scaling their mission.

8. Overcoming Self-Doubt and Confidence Issues

Many female entrepreneurs face self-doubt, particularly in male-dominated industries. However, a growth mindset allows women to push through these feelings of inadequacy. They understand that success doesn't come without setbacks, and that self-doubt can be used as motivation to prove to themselves — and to others — that they are capable.

Purpose plays a significant role here, as it helps female entrepreneurs stay focused on their broader goals. A clear, meaningful mission can fuel their belief in their own potential, making them more confident and determined to succeed.

By infusing their entrepreneurial journey with a growth mindset and a strong sense of purpose, female entrepreneurs are breaking down barriers that once seemed insurmountable. They are transforming challenges into opportunities for growth, innovation, and impact. This mindset allows them to view financial, societal, and personal challenges not as obstacles but as steppingstones toward creating lasting change, not just for themselves, but for the world. Through this combination, female entrepreneurs are not just rising — they are thriving, building businesses that are impactful, sustainable, and empowering others along the way.

Precious Nyarambi

Precious Nyarambi is a dynamic leader and accomplished entrepreneur with expertise spanning technology, medical innovation, and social impact ventures. As the founder and CEO of multiple successful enterprises, she blends strategic vision with a passion for driving meaningful change. A sought-after speaker and author, Precious is dedicated to empowering businesses and startups through her consulting work, guiding them to sustainable success.

Her commitment to philanthropy reflects her belief in giving back and creating opportunities for others. As an alumna of both the prestigious Cherie Blair Foundation and GIBS, Precious brings a wealth of knowledge and a global perspective to every endeavor.

Connect with Precious at https://www.vesselsofvirtue.org.za.

CHAPTER 15

From Corporate Confinement to Empowering Entrepreneurial Dreams

Sara E. Roy

To my three incredible children: You are my why, my
purpose, and the source of my inspiration. May you
always have the courage to follow your own path, the
determination to stand up for what's right, and the
confidence to believe in your limitless potential.

"I'm so disappointed in you and your recent performance." These are the words my director spat at me in his east coast accent. I sat there shaking my head in disbelief as tears spilled down my face. My 18-year-old daughter, overhearing the entire Zoom conversation from the living room, came in to see why her mom was in tears. In over 20 years in corporate America, I had never heard those words spoken to me. Just a week earlier, that same director praised my contributions to the team. Over my nine years with the organization, I received awards and recognition and was nominated for high-performer leadership development programs. What the hell just happened?

Background

It was late May 2022, over two years post-COVID. I had been working remotely from my home in the suburbs of Kansas City and joined a new team five months earlier, in December 2021. I was married with three kids, aged 18, 15, and 12. My then-husband was self-employed running a local in-ground pool construction business, while I was the steady income earner, with benefits, raises, and bonuses—in a position I thought was secure. But in June 2021, everything shifted. My prior team of 15 was laid off as part of a reorganization. People I had worked closely with for almost two years lost their jobs overnight. It was a wake-up call that left me questioning my own career's stability, especially under a new C-suite leader with little empathy or emotional intelligence, whose sole focus was on proving how great he was, even at the expense of others.

In the aftermath, my role changed drastically. I was assigned a product line I had no strategic input into before the reorganization. Though I knew it wouldn't perform well, I was still responsible for its outcomes. I attended countless meetings where my colleagues and cross-functional team members were humiliated and belittled by this leader. We never felt safe or secure in our roles. Every meeting was a gamble—would we encounter Dr. Jekyll or Mr. Hyde or both? As weeks went by, hope for improvement faded, replaced by helplessness and discouragement. Like many colleagues, I began to plan my next move and started the familiar path of searching for a new job.

In December 2021, over the holidays, I updated my resume and began applying to every job I thought I'd qualify for. Despite my 20 years of experience, I encountered rejection after rejection—or, in many cases, no response. I struggled to convey my diverse, transferable skills in a one- to two-page resume, and after two months of searching, I had only two interviews. The feedback was disheartening: I was "too much of a generalist," I hadn't directly led a team, or my salary was far above what prospective employers were willing to offer.

Meanwhile, my current role was deteriorating rapidly, as the product line I oversaw launched and, predictably, failed to perform. While I proposed strategies for improvement to my director, my C-suite leader deprioritized these initiatives, and I lacked the resources to make a meaningful impact. I felt helpless and began to question everything I knew about myself.

The Turning Point

One cold, dreary afternoon in February 2022, I hit a breaking point. I broke down in tears, feeling utterly defeated. My product line was failing, my job search was fruitless, and I was overwhelmed with stress and anxiety about another looming round of layoffs. The pressure was taking a significant toll on my mental and physical health, affecting every aspect of my life, including personal relationships and how I showed up as a mother, wife, and individual. Just as I managed to pull myself together, I received a text from a former colleague who was impacted by the June 2021 layoffs. We'd kept in touch since then, and he had chosen an unconventional path after losing his job: he bought a franchise coaching business through The Entrepreneur's Source (TES)®, a franchise that provides coaching and education services to individuals in career transition who are open to exploring business ownership as an alternative career path for achieving their goals.

When I shared how miserable I was over text, he immediately called and said, "Let's just talk. I can tell you more about what I do and we'll see where it goes." I laughed and responded, "Sure, we can talk, but I will NEVER buy a franchise!" Little did I know, that text and phone conversation marked the beginning of a journey to discovering my true self, my worth, and my future.

In the couple of months that followed, my former colleague and I met weekly over Zoom. He guided me through coaching exercises focused on self-reflection, goal identification, and understanding possibilities in business ownership. He connected me with funding partners, helping me learn about financing options potential business owners often use. He also introduced me to successful businesses in his network, giving me deeper insights into the intricacies of business ownership, including models, operations, marketing, lead generation, and technology.

One of those successful businesses was TES, the very franchise he was part of. This opportunity intrigued me because of my passion for helping people grow and develop. As a project manager by nature, I thrive on evaluating pain points, identifying solutions, and executing plans to effectively address challenges. The idea of owning a remote business where I could work from home without managing employees was especially appealing, given how overwhelmed I'd felt watching the ups and downs of my husband's business. As I continued my coaching sessions with my former colleague and learned more from my TES franchise developer and other TES representatives, I found myself feeling increasingly hopeful about the possibilities ahead.

Through these coaching sessions, I discovered three key insights that changed my perspective. First, business ownership doesn't require a groundbreaking idea or deep expertise in a specific industry. Second, I understood I was my own best advocate. Leaders and managers don't always act in their team's best interest; decisions are often shaped by personal agendas and office politics. A mentor once described the C-suite as a game master, moving key employees around like pawns on a chessboard. Most employees aren't even on the board, but being there is essential for recognition and promotions. Once your usefulness is over, it's "checkmate." I realized I was tired of being someone else's pawn.

Finally, I learned a franchise business was an excellent fit for me. It provided the support and structure I needed to thrive, especially as someone who excels in a project management environment. I knew I couldn't manage all aspects of business ownership alone—I'd seen my husband struggle with it in his business. Without that structure, I'd likely become overwhelmed and focus on the wrong priorities. But with a franchise, I saw a clear path forward.

Oddly enough, I had a lightbulb moment when I realized the organization I worked for operated franchise offices. From a corporate perspective, I already understood the franchise landscape—required disclosures, laws, regulations, corporate support, and even the challenges between corporate and franchisees. Yet, I had never seen myself as a business owner, so the idea of becoming a franchisee and leveraging what I already knew from my organization had never crossed my mind. Sometimes, the answers are right in front of us—we just need someone to help us see them.

Enough is Enough

That reprimand from my director in late May 2022 was the breaking point. As I replayed the entire conversation in my mind, it became clear—he was redirecting his own accountability onto me to save face with the C-suite. He was someone I had trusted, someone I had even felt sympathy for because I knew things hadn't been going well for him. He was just as fearful of losing his job as the rest of us on the team. But when push came to shove, he didn't hesitate to throw me under the bus.

What made the moment truly pivotal, though, was the fact that my 18-year-old daughter—on the brink of adulthood—had witnessed it all. She saw her mother, someone she looked up to, being torn down and blamed for things beyond her control. I wasn't going to allow myself to be anyone's scapegoat, and I certainly wasn't going to set that example for her.

So, I composed myself, contacted Human Resources (HR) to report the incident, and spent the rest of the afternoon combing through emails. Each one was a thread of evidence documenting the events that had led to that day's conversation. I was done taking the blame for someone else's fear and incompetence. It was time to stand up for myself.

The following week, I had a call with my director, who had also reported the incident to HR—his version of it, anyway. I didn't hold back. I called him out, walking him through the email trail and pointing out the meetings I had initially been invited to but was later uninvited from—meetings that still took place without me. I laid it all out, making it clear I knew exactly what he had done. I told him I understood why he shifted blame onto me—he was desperate to save himself—but I wasn't going to sit back and accept being put on a performance action plan.

He never admitted to his actions and stood firm in his claim that I was underperforming. But I didn't let it faze me. I informed him that I had already spoken with HR and requested to be removed from his team as soon as possible. HR immediately began searching for other roles across the organization that aligned with my skill set. I had taken matters into my own hands, refusing to be a pawn in someone else's game any longer.

Best Laid Plans

The events of May 2022 led me to a life-changing decision I never thought I'd make. With the unwavering support of my husband and immediate family, and after weeks of due diligence, financial analysis, research, and in-depth discovery, I accepted the award to join The Entrepreneur's Source (TES) system as a franchise business owner. By June 2022, I had made the commitment, and in early July 2022, I officially signed my franchise agreement.

Transitioning into business ownership was going to take time. I needed to secure funding, establish my business, and handle all the tasks required to get started. In the meantime, I went through the motions at work, completing daily responsibilities where permitted and even interviewing for internal positions I had no intention of accepting. My plan was to remain with the organization until annual bonuses were paid at the end of August 2022, give two weeks' notice, and leave by mid-September to begin my TES training. The bonus was essential—I needed the funds to launch my business and support my family during the initial months before generating revenue.

As August wore on, it became clear I was being phased out. My peers noticed I was no longer invited to planning meetings related to my product line or other strategic initiatives. At the same time, there weren't internal roles worth pursuing, even to create the perception I was transitioning within the organization. My director and the C-suite leader became increasingly anxious and frustrated. They hesitated to assign me meaningful work, knowing I planned to leave the team, but were equally irritated I wasn't contributing much due to their exclusion. It was a standoff, and the tension was undeniable.

Following a candid conversation with my director, I went to HR and voiced my concerns. I explained I was being excluded from meetings and not assigned work, which could easily be misconstrued as underperformance. I provided documentation to support my claims and made it clear I felt they were building a case to fire me. In reality, I was doing everything I could to buy time until my bonus was paid, navigating the situation carefully to ensure I could transition on my terms.

Then, in a miraculous and unforeseen turn of events, HR made me an offer three weeks before I planned to give notice: a full severance package for nearly 10 years of service, with immediate termination. It was an incredible blessing and a no-brainer—I accepted within 24 hours. The severance provided a solid financial foundation, covering much of my business startup costs and easing my transition to entrepreneurship. Two weeks later, another unexpected miracle occurred—I received my annual bonus. Initially, it was only a partial amount, as my director justified a reduction by citing underperformance. However, HR intervened and increased it to 100%. While it fell short of what I deserved for successfully completing a major project in the prior fiscal year, it was enough to give me the runway I needed to move forward confidently.

By mid-September, I started my training with TES, fully committed to my next chapter as a business owner. These miraculous turnarounds marked a fresh start and the culmination of months of resilience, planning, and standing up for myself. It felt like the perfect alignment of events, propelling me toward my new journey with hope and determination.

Today

As for where I am today? I'm over two years into my TES business, and not a single day has passed that I've regretted leaving Corporate America for business ownership. It hasn't been without its ups and downs, but the rewards have been incredible. I own my destiny, and the impact I've made has been life-changing—not just for me but for those I've had the privilege to work with.

In just 3.5 months, I began generating revenue, surpassing the average of 4–6 months. By 2023, I had replicated my corporate income, and by the second quarter of 2024, I exceeded it. Along the way, I've been recognized for my achievements, receiving TES' Rock'n Rookie Award in September 2023 and the Rising Star Award in 2024. My journey has been featured in blogs, podcasts, and a year-long run as a co-host of *Financial Freedom* on the Thriving Women Network.

Through my coaching, I've guided clients to clarity, helping them start businesses and embrace their journeys. I've made lasting friendships with clients and fellow coaches nationwide, built a network, and expanded my influence as a speaker. Most importantly, I've set an example for my children. My now 21-year-old daughter has witnessed my transformation into a confident, strong woman leader and an example of the incredible strength women possess.

It all began with faith in myself—the belief that once I set my mind to something, I would see it through. It took a willingness to embrace the unknown, to learn something new, and the courage to stand up when something wasn't right. The journey hasn't been easy, but my determination and resilience have carried me through every challenge. Today, I'm living proof of the power of self-belief. I'm more fulfilled, more empowered, and making a meaningful difference in my own life and the lives of others.

Sara E. Roy

Sara E. Roy is a dynamic Career Ownership Coach and Business Owner with The Entrepreneur's Source, empowering individuals in career transition to explore entrepreneurship as a viable path to achieve their goals. She specializes in providing no-cost education and coaching on entrepreneurial opportunities, including building passive income streams and diversifying investment portfolios.

Sara's unique coaching approach begins with helping clients articulate their goals, values, and lifestyle aspirations. She provides education on business fundamentals, funding options, and alternative career pathways while offering a supportive space to overcome emotional barriers and embrace the possibilities of entrepreneurship.

In addition to running her business, Sara is deeply involved in organizations that advocate for small business ownership, women entrepreneurs, and women in leadership. As a sought-after speaker, she inspires audiences nationwide on topics related to business ownership and franchising.

Before becoming a business owner, Sara built a 20+ year corporate career in consulting, process improvement, program and project management, product management, and strategic planning. She also completed numerous executive leadership development programs and earned her MBA from St. Mary's University.

Sara resides in the Kansas City Metropolitan area with her three children. She is passionate about creating meaningful experiences with her kids, whether attending sporting events, musicals and concerts, or enjoying outdoor adventures together.

Connect with Sara at https://sroy.esourcecoach.com.

CHAPTER 16

I'm Not a Leader

Sommerville Kimberley Lombard

To my precious Mommy, who walked every step of my
leadership journey with me. Your unwavering love,
encouragement, and belief in my potential have inspired
me to aim higher, be better, and strive to become the person
that you always saw in me. This chapter is for you.

"I'm not a leader." Not a statement you expect from someone who is seen as one, but my leadership journey began with this exact belief. I believe not everyone is born a leader, some of us need to grow into it. Growing from a wallflower into someone who is seen as an authority figure is not easy, but definitely doable.

Starting Out

My journey started at the end of my final year of high school at a private school. I had finally graduated from school, and it felt like a huge weight had been lifted from my shoulders. I am sure everyone can relate to the first day of freedom after graduating. No more homework, no more teachers telling you what you can or especially cannot do! It was exhilarating. But my life changed from that very moment.

I was invited to join the school's personnel as the IT Center assistant. Seeing as I had no other plans after graduating, I thought this was a great opportunity. I graduated and now had an immediate way of earning money. Awesome. Now you see, this shy little wallflower would never have been able to handle going to interviews, let alone having to look for work. I was always the quiet girl in the back row, just watching everyone else, following the rules, and doing my homework. I hated anything close to conflict or disagreement, and always wanted to fit in but never could. So being offered an opportunity to work instantly in the subject I enjoyed the most was like winning first prize in a race. Even though I received this amazing opportunity, I never saw myself as a leader.

This position went well for a few years, and I grew from being a little wallflower to having a bit more confidence in front of a small crowd of young students. I had a great supervisor during those years. She was more of a mentor to me and knew exactly how to build me up and help me grow from the inside out. She eventually left to explore other opportunities, leaving her position open. *"Nope! I am not a leader. This is beyond my capabilities."* Those words constantly ran through my mind. How could I fill such big shoes? Nope, this was not for me.

Rising to the Challenge

I was, again, approached by the school to take on the supervisor position. I was scared! So many more responsibilities, and the prospect of teaching teenagers when I am barely in my 20s — it was petrifying! It took me a while to give them my answer, but I was determined to grow.

I still did not see myself as a leader even though I was in a leadership position. It is a very hard shift to make, transitioning from being a follower most of your life to having a leader's mindset. I would just go through the motions every year ensuring my students always had a good knowledge of Microsoft and its applications. I later grew into teaching basic graphic design and web design to the teens. This was an accomplishment for me because I always feared them, still having that wallflower mentality. This went on for about a decade, when my growth had finally stagnated. The logical thing would be to look for another job with more room to grow. I tried, and tried, and tried but no doors would open. To cut a long story short, which I will one day put into my autobiography, we ended up having to relocate to another part of the country to help my husband's family with their resort.

This relocation meant I had a new pool of opportunities to look through. It took a few months and eventually got a position as a returns clerk in a pharmaceutical warehouse, worlds apart from being a teacher! Though the corporate atmosphere wasn't a good fit, it was a crash course in adapting quickly and finding my voice. After being promoted to dispatch administrator, I recognized the importance of aligning work with passion. I enjoyed this position a lot more but still the cons outweighed the pros. At this point my journey took a drastic turn.

After about a year, I decided this was not for me, and I went looking for other work — to no avail! No doors were opening, AGAIN! Why? Was this going to be the end of me? Am I stuck here, destined to turn into a mindless robot? I couldn't stand the thought of that. I had to make a change. No, I NEEDED to make a change and a drastic one at that. These experiences reinforced that I needed to take control of my career, pushing me toward entrepreneurship, and ultimately my leap into the world of remote work.

The Moment of Transformation

At the end of 2018, I left my job with no backup plan, no way forward besides an idea and a gut feeling! I know this was reckless, but I just knew there was something else out there for me and I was determined to find it.

With only enough savings for three months, I went searching everywhere on the net for work I could do from home. I did not want to work for a boss anymore; I wanted to be the boss. I could be the boss of me, that's not too hard. I tried everything and applied for everything, until one day when I read about being a Virtual Assistant (VA). *"Hey! They are describing me! I think I can do that! That encompasses all my skills and leaves room for growth/learning. Yes, let's do this!"* And so, the next leg of my journey began!

By April of 2019, I had my first client. He was amazing, and still is to this day! It was a learn on the job position. He would teach me what he needed me to do, so that I could build up my skills and experience, while also helping him establish a staff that is accustomed to his way of working. A win-win for everyone. After about 18 months of working for him and a few other non-payers along the way, I discovered something called networking. It's this amazing event where you get to meet a whole bunch of people and share what you do, hoping someone might resonate with you and may want to do business with you. Well, that was what I thought it was about back then.

Once COVID had us all locked down, I began networking over Zoom with this amazing networking group that was just starting up and they had a different mentality for networking. *"Coffee First, Business Later"* was their slogan. In other words, have coffee with someone (even over Zoom) and get to know one another before you even start talking about business. Build that business relationship first. This is what I did. I really dove in and began having Zoom coffees with everyone I could, even if they were overseas. I met some amazing entrepreneurs with whom I am still good friends with today. Through these relationships, I began learning more about business and most of all, myself. I was often asked, *"Where do you see yourself in five years? What will your business look like?"* I honestly could never answer these questions. I had no idea. My life had changed so much in such a short time and so drastically at times, how was I supposed to create goals for myself, let alone my business! *I have always been a follower and not a leader! This mindset is beyond me!* I always had this repeating at the back of my mind.

I sat down with the network owners one day and they asked me these exact same questions. I was honest. I couldn't answer, not for the lack of determination or ambition but for the lack of business knowledge and what was realistically possible on my own. They helped me see what options I had and where I could take my business. Should I grow into an EVA or an OBM? Or I could even attempt being a project manager. This was getting exciting. I could now see a rainbow of opportunities. They eventually became clients of mine and helped my business grow. Trying to build your business on your own, without being part of a good network, is like panning for gold in a stream. If it's just you, you will take a very long time to find gold, but with a good network you have many people searching for gold for you as well. Your chances for success are already much higher, so you do the same for them, increasing their chances too.

Embracing Leadership

Through my leadership journey I was often times put into positions where I was forced to grow and change my mindset. Networking successfully, dealing with clients that don't want to pay, handling difficult people, working with entrepreneurs who have ADHD, these experiences have all contributed to how I have grown. So, after about two years, I decided I wanted to rebrand my business. I wanted it to represent more of me and not just a quick logo I threw together. So, rainbows and hibiscus here we come. I also wanted to incorporate growth in the title, so I called myself an agency — **The Sommerville Agency**. At the time, it was just me in the agency, but it was a constant reminder of the dream. I wanted to be able to help other struggling VAs that were just like me. I want to be able to give them opportunities to earn money so that they could also be their own boss.

I am starting to warm up to the idea now of having someone work for... me. This was an odd thing to say! For me? Really? Just to think it makes my brain bend sideways. This would mean.... Yes, I would need to be a leader. I would have to step up to the plate and be able to delegate the work I was always used to doing for clients. How do I give that up! Will it be done properly like how I would do it? Will the client be dissatisfied and find someone else? Won't it be more work to manage others rather than to just do the work myself! You know these dumb questions and thoughts? The ones that creep up and put you into a state of overwhelm and fear? I was stuck in this rut for quite a while. I tried using other VAs to outsource some of my work, but it just never worked out. I was not ready to step up and be a leader.

Then came along a project where I had to be a project manager. The project ran for six months and ended with a finale where everyone came together for a graduation and "Shark Tank" of sorts. I started this project very shy (as usual) and stayed behind the scenes making sure all the moving parts of the project were running smoothly. I slowly found myself coming more and more to the forefront; giving advice, delegating some tasks, giving more of myself than what was expected. The finale was the cherry on the cake. In that moment, I knew what needed to be done and how it was supposed to get done so that this event would run without a hitch. Obviously, things never go to plan, but successfully pivoting under pressure is what I do best. All obstacles were overcome and to the audience everything went smoothly. Yay, a job well done, and yet this is not the end.

Looking back in hindsight, I see a Sommerville I do not recognise. Was that REALLY me? Did I just do that? I saw someone who was in control of the whole event, from media crew, to MCs, to online and in-person attendees, and even the judges that were there to judge the pitches. She controlled the whole event! Who was this woman? I couldn't believe that was me. She was confident and authoritative in a high-pressure environment. What shocks me the most, is she did it so effortlessly. I can't believe that was me! Do I really have the makings of a good leader? The answer is yes, **yes, I do**!

After this pivotal event, I had a huge shift in mindset. I realized I could be, and I am, a leader now. I needed to make some changes with my new leadership mindset. I started looking for and finding capable VAs that I can successfully outsource tasks to. I have stepped up to the plate to be a VA Agency Owner/Leader. I have some wonderful ladies that I am training to be VAs, so that they too can have their own businesses.

Through LeadHERship Global I have learned so much about business and being a leader in it. Through this, I have broadened my horizons to other leadership opportunities, like writing a chapter in a best-selling book, speaking more in public, and pursuing a position on a board of directors in the next 10 – 20 years.

Not everyone is born a leader, some of us need to grow into it. It has taken me over 20 years to realize I can be a leader despite having been a shy little wallflower.

I realize now that leadership isn't about perfection. It's about growth, service, and lifting others to see their own potential. This is not the end of my journey; it's only the beginning of the next chapter of my leadership journey.

Sommerville Lombard

Sommerville Lombard is a proud mom of three, based in Limpopo, South Africa. She is a Creative Content Specialist, Founder of The Sommerville Agency (VA Services), Lead Generation Coach, a successful course creator, and an Online Project Manager. With 20+ years of teaching experience, specifically in IT and Computer Courses for all ages, she brings a wealth of knowledge and expertise to her work.

As the founder of The Sommerville Agency, a dynamic Virtual Assistant business, she leads a talented team of VAs, providing tailored solutions to help clients grow their businesses. She also serves as the Lead Generation Coach on The Fempreneur Entrepreneur Program, teaching budding entrepreneurs the art of lead generation with practical, results-driven techniques. As an Online Business/Project Manager, Sommerville partners with businesses to support their growth and help them reach their goals.

In addition to these roles, Sommerville specializes in content creation that drives engagement and brand visibility. From designing custom social media graphics and infographics to editing short videos, reels, and presentations, she delivers creative solutions that make businesses stand out. As a GoHighLevel (GHL) expert, she simplifies business processes through CRM setup, funnel creation, automation workflows, and email campaigns, ensuring clients can nurture leads effectively while saving time.

She is also deeply involved in course creation, focusing on developing impactful, interactive, and educational digital learning experiences. Sommerville excels at transforming complex topics into accessible, easy-to-follow formats, empowering learners and entrepreneurs alike.

Connect with Sommerville on LinkedIn at

https://www.linkedin.com/in/sommerville-lombard/.

CHAPTER 17

From the Depths of Despair to Boundless Bliss

Dr. Sonja Jahn, Ph.D.

---

*Dedicated to you – someone who knows that being happy,
at ease and at peace, successful and prosperous, making an
impact, and expressing your true self demands inner work.
It's not always easy, but it's essential. Persist, persevere,
and be patient. It'll pay off in ways you cannot yet imagine.*

"Are you better?"

"No."

"Do you feel the same?"

"No. I actually feel worse. I feel numb. I can't feel my emotions. I feel like I'm walking through life like a robot."

My doctor, a man who had known me for over two decades, paused, looking at me as though I were a puzzle he couldn't quite solve. His pen hovered over his clipboard, caught mid-air between curiosity and concern. "Well, then," he finally said, "let's try something else."

But even as he spoke, a deep, heavy sensation pooled in my stomach – a visceral feeling of dread. Something inside me was screaming, "*No.*" It wasn't fear or rebellion. It was a voice I didn't fully understand at the time, but now recognize as my intuition.

"No," I said firmly. "It's okay. I don't want to try anything else."

He tilted his head, his expression softening. "Are you sure?"

"Yes," I replied, with a conviction that surprised even me.

This wasn't an impulsive decision. It came from a place so deep within me it felt immovable, a place that understood something my rational mind couldn't yet articulate.

Three months earlier, I had walked into this same office, desperate for help. I'd been drowning in feelings of hopelessness, fatigue, and disconnection. Everything felt meaningless. My doctor had explained that I was suffering from depression caused by a chemical imbalance in my brain. He handed me a prescription for a popular antidepressant and assured me, "This will help."

I clung to his words like a lifeline, following his instructions to the letter. But instead of relief, the medication left me feeling worse. The sadness I'd been battling transformed into an unbearable numbness. It was as if my emotions had been sealed off behind a thick, impenetrable wall.

By the time I returned for my follow-up appointment, I knew the medication wasn't the solution. When he suggested trying another type of anti-depressant, my inner voice – so often drowned out by external advice – spoke up loud and clear. This wasn't the answer.

"There must be another way," I thought, even though I didn't yet know what that might be.

"Well, why don't you try therapy?," people suggested, their voices tinged with both concern and insistence.

I had considered it before seeing my doctor. To get a sense of what it might offer, I asked some friends and fellow depressed students who had been seeing a psychologist for six months or more if they were feeling better.

The most common answer was lukewarm at best: "A little." **A little?** That wasn't going to cut it. I wasn't searching for partial relief. I didn't want the edges of my pain dulled; I wanted to be free of it *entirely*.

Others chimed in with less helpful advice: "You'll just have to live with it." **Live with it?** The words echoed in my mind, sparking a quiet rebellion within me. I knew there had to be another way.

Seeing that medication wasn't a solution, therapy was unconvincing, and resignation wasn't an option, I resolved to take matters into my own hands. Depression wasn't just something to endure – it was something to confront, challenge, and ultimately eliminate from my mind and body completely.

And then I had a stroke of good luck…

I developed severe lower back pain!

Journey to Freedom

The pain was debilitating. Desperate for relief, I turned to a friend. Her response was both unexpected and life changing. She handed me a book: *You Can Heal Your Life* by Louise L. Hay.

The book introduced me to the mind-body connection – a radical idea at the time – and it captivated me. I devoured each page, astonished by how accurately it pinpointed the emotional root of my back pain, naming the fear I had buried deep within.

That book became my beacon, leading me down a path of self-discovery and transformation. But the journey wasn't as simple as reading a few pages and magically feeling better. It was a labyrinth, complex, challenging, and often frustrating.

During those pre-Google days, I scoured libraries and bookstores for anything related to the mind-body connection, psychoneuroimmunology, and the emotional roots of physical ailments. One revelation stood out: *my depression was linked to suppressed anger.*

Determined to address it, I signed up for self-development courses that promised to help me deal with my emotions. They taught me to manage, distract from, or intellectualize my emotions. Essentially, they taught me to suppress them.

The relief was fleeting, and deep down, I knew I wasn't addressing the core issue.

A Breakthrough

It became clear that the traditional approaches – medication, distraction-based techniques, intellectual engagement – weren't enough. If I wanted true freedom, I would have to forge my own path.

Armed with knowledge of metaphysics, the mind-body connection, and my own intuitive abilities, coupled with a lot of self-analyses, I embarked on a journey to uncover new ideas and create processes, which I would try out on myself. Some things I tried worked well, others didn't – it was all part of the learning process guiding me closer to the solution.

Six months later, after countless hours of trial, error and success, I finally figured out a process that bypassed the conscious mind and freed me from the subconscious shackles holding me captive.

And just like that, the chains fell away. The darkness lifted. For the first time in years, I felt alive. Lighter and free.

The Existential Crisis

Not only did freedom from depression give me immense relief, peace and (long lost) happiness, it also brought me to the transformative path of personal and spiritual development which I began in all earnestness in 1995.

Two years after I completely freed myself of depression, at the age of 26, I achieved what many would consider a dream: I was appointed director of the Humanities Computing Project at the University of the Witwatersrand. By all outward appearances, I was thriving. I excelled in my role, enjoyed my work, and received a lot of praise. And yet, something felt profoundly absent.

One sunny afternoon, after teaching a class to students, I sat at my computer and thought, "This can't be it. There has to be more to life. We can't leave school, get a degree, find a job, do that job for many years, get married, have children, do that job for another couple of decades, retire and then die."

Cleary the state of ennui (existential boredom) I had slipped into reached a crescendo now, as the thoughts kept echoing in my mind, **"This cannot be it. There has to be more to life than this."**

For one year, I kept asking the Divine:

Why am I here?

What am I meant to do?

What is my purpose?

For months, I heard nothing but silence. Then, I came across a passage in one of Wayne Dyer's books: "When you want something and keep asking for it, it doesn't come. Send out the intention and let it go."

That was my turning point. I released my questions to Source, sent them out like a rocket into the ether and thought, "Let's see what comes back."

Two months later, Source sent the answer – in the form of a postcard.

The moment felt almost cinematic. I was sitting across from a friend at a cozy Italian restaurant, the scent of fresh basil and oven-baked pizza wafting through the air. After our meal, she reaches over to a turnstile by the counter, pulling out a postcard. These postcards were advertisements for products you could buy, or courses you could attend.

With a playful flick of her wrist, she flips it in front of me, saying, "Isn't this for you?"

I look at the postcard and smile. It reads, *Join us for the first Louise Hay teacher training course in South Africa.*

My heart raced. Louise Hay's book, You Can Heal Your Life, had sparked my journey into self-discovery and inner transformation, and now, here was a chance to deepen it.

I eagerly signed up for the prerequisite workshop. An hour in, as the facilitator explains the conscious and subconscious mind and the body-mind connection, I have this moment of absolute clarity. Every fibre of my being is in resonance as I feel, "This is it! This is what I want to do." Source had delivered my purpose.

A few months later, I embarked on the weeklong teacher training, but I wasn't satisfied with just one certification. I immersed myself in dozens of additional courses – from personal and spiritual development to holistic and quantum healing, NLP, energetics, spiritual practices and psychic development.

In the years to follow, I became an internationally certified and accredited Hypnotherapist, Transpersonal Counsellor, Metaphysical Practitioner, Holistic Life Coach and Stress Management Consultant. So enthralled by what I was learning, the academic in me couldn't resist and I decided – for one last time – to further my studies and end my academic career with my sixth (and last!) degree, a Ph.D. in Transpersonal Counseling.

By the time I opened my part-time practice as a counselor and personal development coach in 2000, I intuitively knew I wouldn't follow the 'traditional' approach. I knew deep down that there is a better, more effective way to help people. I made it my mission to develop methods that would completely remove inner limitations and blocks, freeing clients 100% from what held them back in their personal and professional lives. Most importantly, I wanted to ensure these results would last for the rest of their lives.

This was no small task. To succeed, I had to be realistic about my capabilities and limitations, persistent in my efforts, and unyielding in my pursuit. Above all, I needed to be *relentless* in my commitment to what I knew was possible. I stayed laser-focused on my goal, unwavering in my belief that it could be achieved.

The unique, proven methods I've developed so far, the profound inner transformation and lasting results my clients experience are living proof that being a maverick helps you make a valuable contribution to the wellbeing of humanity.

A Leap of Faith

In 2001, life presented me with yet another unexpected opportunity to 'do my inner work' and accelerate my personal and spiritual development. I crossed paths with a South African spiritual teacher who was based in Hawaii and whose mission is to help raise people's consciousness. She invited me to assist her for six months as she traveled across the United States, giving darshan and workshops. Darshan, a Sanskrit word meaning "vision of God," transmits Divine Light into your soul, fostering healing, resolving karma, purifying energy centers, and accelerating spiritual growth.

The invitation was exhilarating. The idea of traveling across the U.S., experiencing more darshans and immersing myself in more transformative work felt like a dream. Without hesitation, I said yes. I resigned from my job at the university and put growing my practice on hold.

What I didn't realize was that the next six months would become one of the most intense purification journeys of my life.

The Purification Process

From August 2001 to February 2002, I traveled across the U.S., assisting the spiritual teacher with darshans and workshops. Within weeks, after receiving several darshans, I felt lighter, more peaceful, and deeply connected to myself. Yet, I was eager to move through my inner challenges faster. At each darshan, I set a powerful intention: *Activate whatever I need to work through.*

The results were swift – and intense. After one darshan, I felt immense pain in my heart chakra. Physically excruciating and emotionally draining, it consumed me every waking moment, sparing me only while I slept.

Desperate for relief, I asked the teacher, "When will this end?"

Her response was simple: **"Go through it."**

It wasn't the answer I wanted. Realizing there was no easy or fast way out, I faced it. For four relentless months, I embraced the pain. I cried. I used the techniques she taught me to process and release my emotions, clearing them out completely.

And each darshan stripped away layers of anger, hurt, fear, and emotional baggage I had carried for lifetimes. This deep, ongoing inner work, coupled with regular darshans, transformed me from within and I felt so much better for it. But I had *no idea* how this would ultimately pay off.

Boundless Bliss

In January 2002, at the final darshan of our U.S. tour, after receiving the blessing, I felt an overwhelming sense of bliss. A while later, when one of the darshan assistants found me, my body was completely paralyzed, yet my consciousness was expanded beyond anything I'd ever experienced. I felt limitless, as though I were no longer confined to my physical form. Joy, peace, and love pulsated through me with an intensity I've never experienced.

When the spiritual teacher arrived to assist, she looked at me with a knowing smile and said: "We'll have to carry her to the car. She's gone into samadhi."

Samadhi has been described as 'a state of God union,' a state of cosmic consciousness which most spiritual masters have said is indescribable.

For 10 hours, I remained in this state of extreme bliss and oneness. Time ceased to exist. Space dissolved. I felt an overwhelming connection to Source, as though I were a single drop in the ocean, feeling the qualities of the ocean, yet not being the ocean.

The Tangible Transformation

Going into samadhi for the first time marked a turning point in my life. I now knew what it feels like to be in communion with the Divine and feel the presence of your soul.

This inner transformation didn't just benefit me; it revolutionized my work with clients. My heightened intuitive abilities allowed me to pinpoint the root causes of their challenges with uncanny accuracy, whether they sat across from me or were 10,000 miles away in a virtual session.

Having this life-changing experience drove home how absolutely vital it is to do your inner work, because so much depends on it.

The Power of Inner Work

Returning to South Africa in February 2002, I met Paramahamsa Vishwananda, a God-realized master who continues to guide me to this day.

The darshans with him brought further experiences of samadhi. Over time, I noticed something profound: layers of unresolved issues continued to dissolve, and my ego was steadily stripped away, revealing my true self – my soul. Feeling my soul's presence within my body – every moment of the day — has transformed my life in ways I never could have imagined.

From this journey, I realized two key truths:

1. Having the grace of a God-realized master in your life is priceless. Their presence can dissolve karma, accelerate your inner transformation, and profoundly ease the path to realizing your true self.

2. The choice isn't **if** you'll face your inner blocks and challenges; it's **when**. Will you choose to deal with them now? In five years? Maybe not even in this lifetime. But eventually, the work must be done.

And when you choose to engage in inner work, *how* you do it matters.

We live in a world that believes "time heals all wounds," – no, it doesn't. And prescribes superficial fixes: "just let it go," and "medicate and move on." But none of these addresses the root cause.

When you want to start, here's how:

1. **Increase your awareness.** Pay attention to your thoughts, emotions, and behaviors. Notice the patterns.

2. **Acknowledge what needs to change.** You can't fix what you don't admit exists.

3. **Take decisive action and persist.** True transformation requires courage and commitment. Find a well-respected expert with a proven track record of deep, lasting transformation who can help you clear the mental and emotional blocks – not partially, but completely.

Why is it so absolutely vital to do your inner work?

Because so much of what you want depends on it: a fulfilling relationship, enhanced business success, increased prosperity and impact, as well as feeling happy, calm and at peace.

And perhaps most importantly, you'll realize your true self – the part of you that is whole, peaceful, and radiant.

As Paramahamsa Vishwananda so beautifully says, "Help yourself first, then you'll be able to help others. When you have changed, it will be a blessing to you and everybody else."

Dr. Sonja Jahn, Ph.D

Dr. Sonja Jahn, Ph.D., H.LC, C.Ht., CSMC is a well-respected transformation specialist, holistic life coach, metaphysical practitioner, transpersonal counselor, and hypnotherapist with a remarkable 25-year career helping entrepreneurs, leaders, and changemakers worldwide break free from mental barriers, unwanted emotions, and self-limiting behaviors, empowering them to thrive both personally and professionally.

With six degrees under her belt, including a Ph.D. in Transpersonal Counseling, and a foundation in psychology and metaphysics, she blends her highly developed intuitive abilities with her proven Finally Free™ system to help her clients eradicate the subconscious root cause of mental and emotional blocks, enabling them to overcome life's challenges – easily and effectively.

The results of her work are life changing. Clients report a profound, lasting inner transformation that radiates through every aspect of their lives. They cultivate deeper, more harmonious relationships, radiate confidence, rediscover joy, and align with a renewed sense of purpose and fulfillment.

This inner freedom enables them to elevate their income, amplify their impact, and accelerate their personal, professional and spiritual growth.

Throughout her career, Dr. Sonja has observed how profoundly our inner world shapes our outer reality and when we decide to free ourselves from inner challenges, we don't just thrive – we become a powerful force for positive change in the world.

Explore her one-time transformative sessions, coaching programs, and workshops to embark on your path to freedom at https://www. drsonjajahn.com.

CHAPTER 18
Becoming Un-invisible

Susan Smalley

To my Mom, Nancy, and "my guy," John. I hope you are dancing to Elvis together.

It's 1985. I'm a junior in college. My roommate and I are at a total dive bar. Even for a college town, it's pretty rank. We are drinking our favorite drink, Jim Beam and Tab. The smell of stale beer and cigarette smoke is palpable. We are having a blast.

A friend of hers sees us and walks over. "Susie meet my friend John, John meet Susie." We look at each other and something sparks. I feel it down to my toes. Instant attraction. He proceeds to keep us entertained and laughing for the rest of the night. "We are the World" is at the top of the charts, and he is doing his best Bob Dylan and Michael Jackson impressions. He is completely charming, full of charisma. It is love at first sight. I never believed in that before, but now I know it's true. We are inseparable after that night. He is "my guy" and I am "his girl."

My Picture-perfect Life

John is the definition of fun and adventure. We always have something fun planned: road trips, football games, or dinner with friends. We laugh our way through the rest of college, move to Atlanta, get married, and eventually land in California, buy a house, and start a family. We are the perfect couple living the perfect life. Friends tell me when they find their partner they want to have a relationship like ours.

My neighbor in California tells me "When I first moved in, I saw you outside with the kids freshly bathed, in their jammies, you were pushing them in the swing and laughing in the front yard. I thought to myself, 'What an idyllic scene. What a perfect family.'"

So, there you have it, my picture-perfect life.

Beautiful house complete with a white picket fence — check.

Two amazing kids — check.

Great job at Disney Studios — check.

John working in the film business — check.

Perfect story, right?

Except it wasn't.

Ok let's back up a few years, I'm getting ahead of myself.

Learning the Code

I was born and raised in the South — Georgia, Tennessee, Alabama were home to me. This is where I learned the unwritten code for women and girls:

1. Be nice. Don't make waves.

2. Look good on the outside. What others think is more important than what you feel.

3. Put others first. Put yourself last.

In short, Be nice. Look good. Put yourself last. I call it "Jazz Hands" because after all, "It's showtime, folks." I learned the code daily — at school, at home, with friends, on TV — basically everywhere. This code became the basis for my decision-making about most things.

Living with Jazz Hands

John and I were both high energy and loved to have fun. His version was a bit more "be the center of attention" and mine was a bit more "let's all have fun together." As time went on, his need to control the conversation and be the center of attention continued to grow. My response was to pull away and become smaller, quieter, and more invisible. Although it didn't feel that great to me, I was following the code. Everything looked good on the outside and everyone else seemed happy, so what else could *I* possibly want or need? I didn't have the words or justification at the time to express what was going on for me, much less what I needed.

This pattern continued for years, becoming more distinct, and more imbalanced. I started to become bitter about the dynamic and didn't know how to verbalize what was going on. I just thought I wasn't happy with John anymore and blamed him.

Here's a glimpse into my world at that time. It's a typical Saturday night. We have several friends over for dinner. Everything is perfect. I have cleaned the house, put out fresh flowers, and made all the side dishes. John's job is to be in charge of the steak. As our friends arrive, the conversation is all about the steak: what cut it is, how it was marinated, and how it is going to be cooked. At the dinner table: how great the steak is cooked; how wonderful it tastes and so on and so on and so on…. This is a metaphor for my life. Now don't get me wrong, the steak *was* so delicious and who doesn't like a good foodie conversation? My struggle is that I am invisible, and my contribution to the night is also invisible. It's not that I want to be the center of attention. It just becomes all about my partner and no room for anything else. It is awkward and frustrating for me especially because everyone else is having a blast. I don't know how to talk about it without feeling selfish or silly or breaking the code, so I continue to feel invisible… for years.

Be nice. Look good. Put yourself last. "Jazz Hands."

My Wakeup Call

We continue to spiral down, until one morning I look in the mirror and realize I do not recognize the person I have become. A resentful, bitter, invisible woman who has lost her sparkle. I know there is more to life than self-pity, and this is not the way I want to continue. I decide in that moment I will change my life. I will find my voice and my sparkle. I have so much more to give and so much more to become. I know in order to do that I need space from my partner so I can relearn how to show up and be seen. This is my own journey, and although my voice is there, it will not be easy to break the code, lose the "Jazz Hands" to get to my truth and deeper knowing. AND I also remember thinking, "Girl, take a deep breath. You got this. And let's not forget who you are — remember you're Susan Fucking Smalley! You can do this, SFS."

So, John and I separated. As he is walking out the door, I say to him, "I'm not *against* you, John. I'm *for* me." And that has never been more true than at that moment.

I was working part time, so I knew I needed to find full time work. After a long search, I made the extremely unbelievable decision to quit my job and start my own coaching and leadership development business. Talk about a leap of faith — within one year I had left my husband of 20+ years and my job of 15+ years. I was creating the life of my choosing, with no one to rely on but myself, no partner, no team, no boss, no parents. It was all me, and that is what I needed it to be for now. I was excited, terrified, and completely dedicated to becoming a better, stronger, more confident person through this journey. My goal was to find and trust my voice, no more being invisible. Less "Jazz Hands." More "SFS."

I remembered that a friend used to marvel at how I could change myself to fit in with any crowd. She called me a chameleon, and she thought it was great. I did too at the time. What I see now is that it was the opposite of being true to myself and being authentic. It was another version of "Jazz Hands." I vowed not to be that chameleon anymore as well. Less "chameleon." More "SFS."

Steps in the Right Direction

It's 2016. John and I end up divorcing. Anyone who has gone through a divorce knows that it's no walk in the park. We had a bad habit of exchanging tough messages through text. I'm not proud of some of the things I said to him, and I'm sure he would say the same. One text he sent was particularly excruciating for me, something about not being a great mom, blah blah blah. But this time, the work I was doing on myself, and my voice was paying off. Instead of shooting back an equally horrible reply to him, I paused and responded by not responding. *Yet.*

For days after, whenever I would look at his text, if I got angry, I would put the phone down and not respond yet. I let him have it in my thoughts, but I didn't text him. I yelled at him in the car by myself, but I didn't text him. It took me two weeks before I could read the text and not feel any emotions about what was written. That is when I finally *chose* to respond with "You may be right, John, parenting is hard, and I have not always done it perfectly. You have made your fair share of mistakes too. And if you ever want to discuss anything, I am always willing. With that said, I do not ever want to receive a text like that again, or we will not communicate anymore."

After sending that text, I have never felt more empowered or proud of myself. My response actually changed our dynamic, and we didn't send mean texts to each other anymore after that.

Redefining the Code

Through this process, I am choosing how I want to show up in the world. I am revising what I have been taught since childhood and figuring out my version of the code.

"Be nice. Don't make waves." is becoming, "Be kind and take no shit." Because I'm worth it.

"Look good on the outside." is becoming, "Do what feels good to me on the inside." And sending that text felt really good on the inside.

"Put others first. Put yourself last" is becoming, "Identify my own needs and feelings first. Make them equally (and sometimes more) important than others' needs." And believe it or not, because this one is so foreign, I have a chart that helps me identify them in the moment.

Step by step, I am learning how to listen to my inner wisdom and trust that voice. It is hard work, two steps forward, and one step back, but I am doing it. Slowly but surely, I am rewriting the code. I'm retiring my chameleon. I'm taking off my "Jazz Hands."

Embracing the Journey

It's 2019. John has died. The kids and I host his celebration of life at our home. We include all of the most important people in our lives, his family, my family, his high school friends, our friends from college, Atlanta, and California. We have tables and chairs in the backyard, beer in the cooler, football on the TV, and barbecue cooking on the smoker. A real southern throwdown. I get up to speak to the group. In my speech, I talk about what a great man he was and share some heartfelt and funny stories. We all laugh and cry together a lot, which is as it should be.

When I think about that moment, I am so proud because it signifies the person I have become. I am no longer a resentful, invisible woman. I am a compassionate and authentic woman who is continuing to find my voice and use it for good. I am beyond grateful for the journey and for the people along the way, including "my guy," whose own struggles led me to this better version of myself.

Supporting Other Women on Their Journey

Because of my own journey, I am passionate about working with other women to find and trust their voices. In my coaching and leadership development work, this has become a key component of my work with women at all levels in the organization. As I have shared my story, I have discovered that most women have their own version of "Jazz Hands." After all, most of us learned a version of this code growing up. Whether I'm coaching individuals or groups, speaking at conferences, or leading my women's leadership program, the topic of finding your voice usually comes up. The good news is that once we are aware, we can shift our mindsets and build the skills we need to presence ourselves. We *can* rewrite the code. Supporting others in doing that has become my life's passion and purpose.

Lessons for Reinvention

Here are three of the many lessons I have learned:

1) Don't go it alone. We need support along this difficult path. Find connection and support in as many places as you can: friends, therapists, support groups like Al-Anon, coaches, etc. The more the merrier, but make sure you have at least one.

2) Find time and space to listen to the voice of your inner leader through meditation, walking, journaling, or any creative process etc. You will find that if you create space and really listen, you always know the answer.

3) Take on a growth mindset which reminds you that with effort you can do anything. And remember if you are uncomfortable with something new, that is a sign of growth so hang in there. You just don't know it YET, and you can learn.

Owning my Voice

Here is the bottom line.

I own my voice and my experience. I don't need to wait to be invited to share my needs or my perspective. I don't need permission. That's the old code, that's "Jazz Hands." The new code puts me square in charge of owning my own experience — that's on me. I am responsible for identifying my needs and getting them met. I am responsible for showing up with my perspective and opinions, speaking up about my feelings, and allowing myself to be seen. That is my part. There is vulnerability and hard work in breaking the code. The good news: when I remember who I am, it becomes a little easier because, after all, I am SFS!

Susan Smalley

Susan Smalley, PCC, CPCC is a leadership coach and master facilitator with 20+ years of experience supporting the growth and development of leaders and teams. Her mix of optimism, straight talk, and humor allows her to quickly connect and build trust with her clients.

She is the Founder/CEO of Essential Leadership Partners, specializing in Leadership Development, Team Building & Communication, and Women-Centered Development. She serves her clients through coaching individuals and groups, speaking at conferences, leading team offsites, and teaching leadership skills through her training programs.

She is a lifelong learner and is currently pursuing a certification from the Institute of Women-Centered Coaching.

Susan brings a wealth of real-world experience to her work, spending 15 years at the Walt Disney Studios in leadership development.

Susan lives in her happy place, Long Beach, California, with her two teenagers who still have no idea what she does.

Connect with Susan at https://elpartnersgroup.com.

CHAPTER 19

From Not Good Enough to Have the Power to Create

Susanne Ekström

I'm 16 years old. I love basketball and I play every day. I want to play as a guard, but my coach tells me to play center because I'm tall. He doesn't explain to me why I can't play guard, and I slowly start to perform worse and worse because I feel I am not good enough.

I now have low self-esteem, I feel anxious about going to training, and I am no longer motivated to play.

One day I withdraw and leave the team and never come back. I never play basketball again.

In 2001, I'm on the top of the world. I'm one of the owners of a large Swedish dot.com. We are almost 400 people and established in 10 countries. I'm flying all over the world and I live in the Netherlands, where I'm starting up our Dutch office.

I'm heavily invested in this company — with sooo much passion, time, energy, and money.

During a holiday week skiing in the Alps, a colleague calls me and says that our company has suspended payments. I sit in the ski lift in the sun and behind my sunglasses the tears flow down my cheeks.

A couple of weeks later, our CEO files for bankruptcy.

In the blink of an eye, my whole world falls apart hard and fast. I lose everything, and I'm devastated. Going from a total dream job to no job at all.

I invested so much time, commitment, joy, and money in this company. I had thought — a little naively — that it would somehow work out, that we would get more money from our investors.

I am now without a job, without an apartment (because I live in a flat in the Netherlands that the company pays for) and have large convertible loans in a completely useless company. I feel devastated and disappointed in both myself and my management colleagues for failing to fix this.

But what did we do wrong?

It takes a while for the bankruptcy and all the things we did and didn't do to sink in. I realize the company essentially went bankrupt due to the fact that we didn't have defined processes and clear/functioning communication. The company struggled with productivity problems; we constantly "put out fires," and at last one of these fires caused the company to burn to the ground.

To summarize, we as a company made these four epic failures! We:

✗ Failed to delegate properly

✗ Failed to setup to scale successfully

✕ Failed to create consistent ways of working

✕ Stopped listening to our people as the management team

In that crash, I realize something vital for myself. Even if my company can "sink," I will still survive. I'm a problem solver, not a quitter, so I got back up, and moved home to Sweden to find a new opportunity within the management consulting industry.

I'm now back in my hometown. One day on the way home from meeting a client, it dawned on me that every company I've worked with has had the same problems, regardless of their size or field (including the company that went bankrupt).

How was it that I just realized this now after working all these many years?

Working in a company is the same as playing basketball, just a little more complex.

You can play in different ways:

— Either you have a team where everyone throws their own ball toward the basket or maybe to each other because you have no idea how to play the game.

✚ Or you have a team that is synchronized and motivated, that likes to play together and knows who does what, when, and why.

You need to have a set of basic rules and a strategy for how to play the game. You need a team that knows their goals, that is willing to do the job, and a great coach/team leader who both leads and supports the team.

If you have a team that is not synchronized, you will perform poorly, and you may even be able to get a ball in your head.

Learnings

In basketball, a winning team needs a skilled coach and a strong culture.

The same applies in business: without either, even the best strategies won't make the cut.

A great coach, like a good leader, doesn't just TELL their team what to do — they ASK the team what they think we should do. Listening to your team, sharing your vision, and keeping everyone's focus is crucial to attracting and retaining the best.

I often say, 'culture eats strategy any day' (thanks, Peter Drucker, for that fantastic quote), and if you do not listen to your team about their ideas, problems, etc., you will not win so many games.

And - that's what my basketball coach didn't do. He didn't ask me for my opinion. Due to poor leadership, he let a motivated team player become increasingly unmotivated and finally leave the team to never play basketball again.

I deeply regret not speaking up to my coach all those years ago, but I didn't know how to or what to say. And I learned an invaluable lesson about leadership and communication — the hard way.

I learned the **value of asking** the right questions and **listening carefully** to the answers.

Apart from the basketball analogy, my clients are also teaching me that:

- We're doing a lot of great projects that are often never fully implemented.

- Management doesn't listen to their people, mainly because of lack of time, focus, interest, or self-confidence.

- People don't use their potential within the company anymore. Maybe they've tried, but no one listened... so they're frustrated and just do their job. Nothing more.

- There's often a gap between the management and the employees. The management thinks that they have an outstanding company culture, but in reality it's something completely different.

Not being good enough

Since the basketball "failure," I always tell myself I'm not good enough. In some way, this thought is a shield or excuse not to take action — to hide behind.

💬 It doesn't matter if I call this prospect; he seems to be doing great. What can "little I" offer him?

💬 I'm doing great, but it takes much longer than I thought.

💬 It doesn't matter if I speak up in this meeting; everyone must already have thought about what I'm thinking.

I make up excuses and stories to "prove" and "be right about" my thoughts of not being good enough. All the times that my thoughts were proven wrong don't count. I immediately find something else to prove I'm right.

I hear this is a survival method. But, HEY, survival of what?

I also see that a specific type of woman makes me shy and withdrawn. I notice they remind me of someone from school, Vicky, the toughest girl in class, with whom I've had horrible experiences. On default, I tell myself, "Oh, she's a Vicky."

I remember an incident in fourth grade, in school, and on a break. Vicky dragged me into the toilet and said, "There's no idea that you're in love with Jonas because Jonas is in love with me!" I realize that my brain, in that incident, made this *silly sentence* mean so much more than the actual words.

- Looking back at my relationships, I can see a clear theme — safe, secure, and not extraordinary because I'm not good enough for the men I want.

- Since that weekend course on personal development a year and a half ago, I focus a lot on my mindset and what I tell myself. It's time to get rid of these old thoughts and complaints about me not being good enough.

- For example, that "horrible" memory with Vicky is not affecting me anymore because I see it for what it was, nothing more than a sentence of words from one person to another. My brain made it mean something much "bigger" than the actual words. Now I smile when I realize someone reminds me of Vicky.

And, of course, I'm good enough! 🐝

My entrepreneurial journey – the power to create

In 2017, at the age of 46, I start my own company.

Up until now, working in the management consulting business for 20+ years, I have worked with clients of different sizes and in various industries helping them identify the cause of their problem, issue, or bottleneck causing frustration and irritation. Then, we design a solution, implement it, and further improve it in the most suitable way, ultimately helping them master operational excellence.

My approach and drive are to work with clients in addressing their problems, issues, and ideas with the goal of working smarter, better, and more efficiently. Unlike most other companies, my strategies are completely different. I ask questions, listen to their answers, and find out which problem is the most important to fix first. This problem might not be the problem that the management sees. The most important problem is often something that the employees see. By helping the company focus on the right problem, you get the buy-in from the company culture and you train it to be a vital part of building a better tomorrow for the company.

This has been my "red thread" throughout my journey since 2001. It's the one thing that has brought me lots of joy, exciting assignments, and management roles within the companies I've worked for.

During the pandemic, I shifted the intention of my company and I created the vision of "going international," coaching CEOs, and my brand promise is to "Bring inspiration and innovation to leaders in this world!"

Now, I coach CEOs in building their company's better tomorrow.

A winning company:

- Where all roles (and individuals) are equally important.

- With sustainable, streamlined ways of working.

- Where the extra money on the bottom line is just one of the many results showing that this is a successful company with a championship-caliber team.

Challenges

My first challenge within my new company is finding a client base to help me create revenue and the baseline for building my company's 'digital real estate.'

Work-life balance is also an issue. As a single mom, it is hard to make everything work — both workwise and familywise.

I have also discovered that my youngest son, who is 18 years old, has both ADHD and autism. This has added another level of complexity to my parenthood. He is at home 24/7, not attending school, not participating in any social activities, and we're pretty much stuck in this situation.

This is a total catastrophe for me. I can't get my own son to leave the house. He is just there in his room — on a sort of "strike" from life and I have to bribe him to get him outside.

During a weekend course on personal development, it hits me hard. I want to FIX my son! Because this is NOT the life I was supposed to have. And I'm the reason we're stuck!

Even if we have a fantastic relationship, something needs to change. I need to shift the way I speak and listen to him. I realize I listen to him through a "filter."

After the course, I now focus on what's important to him (not to me). This shift in focus leads him to move to a specialized boarding school and restart his life. He's happy, has friends, and he goes to school. Instead of four years behind in school, he's only one year behind.

Any mom wants to have their kids close to them and helping him move two hours away from me is hard. But I know he has more people in his life who care about him, and he gets the help and support he really needs that I alone can't fully provide.

Building my personal brand

During the first years of running my own company, I got by very well, but I'm not happy with how I put in a lot of hours on things that didn't bring my consulting clients the real value I could provide. I'm often drained of energy by the end of each day.

I see a business model that's not sustainable or scalable value-wise and time-wise and I want to bring the best value I can to my clients more efficiently. Instead of doing it approximately 30% of the time, I want to do it 100% of the time. I want to create leverage via my coaching of the CEO throughout the organization instead of being there myself to cause it.

I assign three different mentors in the following areas

- Building my digital real estate
- Designing my message and target audience
- Speaking and writing business English

I do paid ads on Facebook/Meta and build my personal brand on LinkedIn.

My focus is CEOs of SME companies (Small and Medium-sized Enterprises) on the US East Coast, Canada, and Europe. But why is this Swedish lady targeting the US and Canada? The mindset around the importance and value of a coach differs in the US and Canada from the rest of the world. And I also love to speak English.

It's never too late to start new things.

"I have never tried that before, so I think I should definitely be able to do that." ~Astrid Lindgren, Pippi Longstocking

---

I try to live by this quote, which has, on the one hand, led me to suffer from imposter syndrome throughout my professional life but also led me to be able to grow, both personally and business-wise, in ways that I'm very proud of today.

Susanne Ekström

Susanne Ekström is a visionary entrepreneur, worldwide CEO coach, and the brain behind BeASmarterLeader and SEE Management.

Her goal? Coaching SME CEOs to build winning companies where people love to work.

She has a signature coaching program called "Boost you bottom line by $499k. Delivered in 99 days."

In the past five years, Susanne has helped her clients make over $30 million more in profit. Her signature programs and coaching have transformed more than 6,000 individuals into Smarter Leaders.

Her mission? To guide CEOs like you in reaching the top of your game. She specializes in turning your big business dreams into reality, making your company richer, your team happier, and your business more robust.

To achieve this mission, Susanne focuses on three main areas:

- Freeing up time for you and your key people to strategize.

- Utilizing and optimizing your company's potential for greater productivity and profitability.

- Designing a scalable business model to 2X – 3X your company.

Why? In 2001, her dot-com company went bankrupt during the market crash. This tough experience led her to guide others for over 20 years to avoid similar problems.

Connect with Susanne at https://www.beasmarterleader.com.

CHAPTER 20

Dreams Beyond Boundaries

Vera Firman

I dedicate this chapter to my mother. Without her, I wouldn't be who I am today. She has always believed in me and supported me unconditionally.

Who I Am and the Origins of My Dream

My name is Vera Firman, and I come from a small town called Kerch, a modest city in Crimea — formerly Ukrainian but now a Russian territory. For most of my life, the town I grew up in was little more than a dot on a map. It was remote and quiet, situated between the Black and Azov Seas. However, recent world events have brought Crimea into the global spotlight, a twist I could never have anticipated while growing up.

From an early age, I dreamed of entrepreneurship. I didn't come from a family of business owners or anyone who encouraged that path, so perhaps that desire was fueled by a longing to be different, to break free from the limitations of my environment. Growing up in a place with few opportunities, I wanted more. I wanted to see the world and build something of my own, a legacy that would defy my modest upbringing.

My grandmother noticed this spark in me before anyone else. "You'll be a businesswoman one day," she said when she found out that I was selling my baby clothes to neighbors and collecting glass bottles to recycle for small change. (PS: I was embarrassed to do this and tried to hide from my friends). I was 10 years old at the time, but my grandma's words stayed with me, echoing in my mind whenever I doubted my dreams or felt the weight of what I was trying to accomplish.

Those dreams didn't fade as I got older. In fact, they grew. As I set my sights on places like the United States, a world away from Kerch, I began my journey into a life filled with risk and uncertainty.

Early Influences and Core Values

Growing up in Crimea in the 1990s was quite an experience. The Soviet Union had collapsed, and the region was struggling with economic turmoil. Crime was prevalent, and we were often faced with empty store shelves. My parents would get paid in coupons that are then exchanged for food items, and there were times my dad got paid in canned goods — yep, for real. I remember those days with a wry smile now, but it wasn't funny at the time.

Yet, in the midst of all that scarcity and unpredictability, my family found a way to make life joyful. Those were challenging times, but they taught me invaluable lessons about adaptability, managing resources, and the importance of community.

Sadly, that environment also came with misguided beliefs about wealth and success. In our town, anyone who ran a business was labeled

"Mafia" or suspected of dishonesty. It was an unfortunate reality in post-Soviet society, where success was often seen through a lens of suspicion and envy. This mentality weighed on me as I started on my entrepreneurial journey, creating self-doubt that lingered long after I left my country.

Still, the desire to break free of these limitations was powerful. I wanted to travel, to live abroad, and to create a life on my own terms. This drive led me to take a leap that changed everything: at 20 years old, I left my country for Dubai, an unfamiliar city with a vastly different culture and language.

Taking the First Steps: Moving Abroad and Building Resilience

Dubai was a city of contrasts and opportunities; a vibrant, ultramodern metropolis where I could carve out my path. Arriving with limited English, I was absolutely clueless but also fearless — as most of us are in our twenties. I had no clear plan and knew very little about the culture. Yet, I trusted my instincts. I enrolled in university and took various courses to improve my English. Each day was a challenge, but it was also a step closer to building the life I had always envisioned.

Throughout those early years, I was fortunate to find mentors, people who took me under their wing, offering guidance and support. Most of my friends were older, and from them, I gained knowledge and wisdom that became invaluable as I grew in my career. Dubai became a second home, a place where I could see my dreams begin to take shape, though the path was far from easy.

Working in a foreign country, trying to speak a new language, and striving to fit into an unfamiliar culture taught me resilience. There were moments when I questioned my decisions, but I kept going, each challenge adding layers to my fortitude and sense of purpose.

Early Ventures and the Road to Self-Discovery

My first real attempt at entrepreneurship happened when I was 24 and going through a turbulent time. Stuck between battling with a divorce from my first husband and wanting to support my mother back in Crimea, I opened a small jewelry shop in Kerch. This started as a physical shop, but I moved it online during the e-commerce boom of the early 2010s. It was my first taste of business ownership, a modest shop selling imported jewelry from China. I chose jewelry because I figured it was "safe." It was a non-perishable product that would be unaffected by seasonal changes. Little did I know. The demands of running a business, even a small one, were far greater than I anticipated.

Running the shop remotely from Dubai while juggling a corporate job wasn't easy, but I was determined to make it work. For nearly four years, I managed to keep it afloat. I hired a team and relied heavily on my mother, who was the lifeline of day-to-day operations. Eventually, I had to let it go, the demands of my corporate job and studies became overwhelming, and I realized that managing a business remotely wasn't sustainable — not at that stage of my life anyway. Still, this experience was pivotal, and it taught me the importance of people management and adaptability. Most importantly, it taught me that failure was merely a steppingstone toward my next venture.

Transformative Moments: Growth, Setbacks, and Family

A significant turning point in my life came during my second pregnancy. My corporate job announced that they were closing their Dubai office, and for the first time in my corporate career, I found myself at a crossroads. Financially, my husband and I were stable, and everyone around me suggested I take a break. But I had a burning desire to build something of my own; relying solely on my husband's income wasn't an option as I wanted to create my own security, independence, and legacy.

With the encouragement of a close friend, I took a leap and co-founded a consulting company in Dubai. The journey was full of challenges, from navigating local regulations to building a clientele. Despite the hurdles, the business grew, and today, it continues to thrive, with a team of 20 and a prime office location in Dubai.

The experience reinforced my belief in persistence and grit, especially when things get tough. Motherhood, marriage, and business are often painted as opposing forces, but I believe that they fuel each other. My children became my inspiration, and every challenge I faced hardened my resolve to provide them with a life I could only dream of as a young girl.

In 2020, my family made another life-altering decision: we moved to Portugal, hoping to create a simpler, slower-paced life for our children. The timing was really funny because almost immediately after, the pandemic hit. Like countless others, I found myself in a state of uncertainty, unsure how this would impact the Dubai consulting business. However, in the middle of all the chaos and unpredictability, my mind went back to a long-standing dream: building a business in the United States. On the back of our success in the consulting scene in Dubai, I felt a strong desire to create something new, a digital agency that would allow me to connect with clients from the USA.

Starting an agency in the US was daunting. I was met with skepticism due to my accent and foreign background, and I faced rejections from clients who preferred to work with local and more-recognised firms. But this didn't deter me, rather, it fueled my determination. I poured my energy into learning, networking, and honing my sales skills. Today, VF Agency stands among the top SEO agencies in the US, a success I once thought impossible. But that's not all, I decided to go even further and established a company, called Pulse Growth, that helps businesses streamline and automate their marketing process. Pulse Growth white labels a cool CRM and its value proposition is helping entrepreneurs discover shortcuts and smart tools that set them up for success.

Advice to Women Hesitating to Start Their Dream Business

Starting a business is an act of courage, and for many women, taking that leap feels overwhelming. But if you're hesitating, know that every successful entrepreneur began with the same doubts and fears you have. Here are some lessons from my own experience to help you overcome that hesitation and set yourself up for success.

1. **Discipline Yourself — It All Starts with You:** Discipline is the backbone of any successful business. I've seen it countless times: without a disciplined approach, it's easy to lose focus and direction. Set clear routines, establish goals, and follow through with consistency.

2. **Prioritize Your Health and Well-being:** This may seem secondary, but trust me, it's crucial. Start exercising, eat well, and make time for mental rest. Building a business demands high energy and mental resilience. There were times when I pushed myself to exhaustion, ending up with migraines and back pain from neglecting my health. Remember, if you don't take care of yourself, your business will struggle too. You are the foundation, make sure you're strong.

3. **Learn to Say No — Set Boundaries Early:** One of the biggest challenges I faced at the start of my business journey was saying "yes" when I shouldn't have, from extra responsibilities to unrealistic client demands — simply to avoid disappointing my customers. I did this for too long, and it led to burnout and

frustration. Saying "no" is a form of self-respect and a necessity for protecting your energy. Set your boundaries and stay firm, it will serve you well in the long run.

4. **Document Your Journey — Build SOPs and Systems:** This is key to scaling your business smoothly. Document everything, from daily operations to client processes, and create SOPs (Standard Operating Procedures). Use social media to record your progress and don't wait to start or worry too much about what people will say or think. One of my regrets to date is "why did it take me so long to start doing this." Don't make the same mistake!

5. **Delegate What You Don't Enjoy Doing:** You don't have to do it all, nor should you. Identify the tasks that drain you or that you aren't particularly skilled at and delegate them. And not just in business, if you need help with your kids, hire a nanny. If you don't like cleaning, get someone to do it for you. Don't feel guilty about it, delegation isn't a sign of weakness, it's a strategic move to focus on what you're best at.

These are not just strategies to succeed in business as a woman, they are lifelines that helped me build the life I want while maintaining my sanity and sense of self. So, if you're hesitating, take a step forward. The world needs more women who dare to lead and create boldly.

Legacy and Vision for the Future

As I reflect on my journey, I often ask myself what legacy I hope to leave behind. For me, it's about much more than business success or financial achievements. My true desire is to empower other women to pursue their dreams, no matter where they come from or the challenges they face. I want to set an example of resilience, adaptability, and courage; a testament to what can be achieved when you dare to step beyond cultural limitations, societal expectations, and even your own self-doubt.

When I think back to the young girl daydreaming about a better life in Crimea, I see the spark that has carried me through every stage of my life. That same spark exists in women all over the world, even in the most remote and challenging circumstances. I want my story to be a reminder that where you start does not have to define where you end up.

It's especially important to me to inspire women from all backgrounds, not just those with access to resources or privilege. Whether you're a woman from a small town like I was, someone battling cultural expectations, or simply afraid to take the first step toward your dreams, know this: your background is not a limitation, and your circumstances are not your destiny.

Final Reflections and Encouragement

Looking back, I can see how each hardship and success combined to shape my vision. I hope to empower women who, like me, may feel uncertain or out of place in the business world. I want to show that no dream is too big and that with courage and resilience, even the most unconventional paths can lead to success.

Starting anything new is scary. Fear is natural. It's the mind's way of protecting us from failure, but it can also hold us back from reaching our full potential. My advice? Start anyway. If any cool thoughts or ideas come to your mind, act on them straight away. Don't put them on a shelf and think "I'll just do it later" — why not now? Because you're scared? Do the things that scare you, because fear is often an indicator that what you're about to do is significant. There were countless moments when fear tried to stop me: moving to Dubai with no plan, starting my first business, and even pitching my agency to skeptical clients in the US. But I've learned that courage isn't the absence of fear, it's acting in spite of it.

Setbacks and failures are inevitable, but they are also some of the greatest teachers. When my jewelry shop didn't work out, I could have let it define me as a failed entrepreneur. Instead, I chose to see it as an invaluable lesson in people management, adaptability, and perseverance. Failure isn't a dead end, it's a redirection. Each setback I've faced has been a steppingstone to something greater, and I hope to inspire other women to view their challenges in the same way.

In a world that often tells women to play it safe, I want to be a voice that encourages bold leadership. Women are powerful agents of change, capable of leading industries, shaping communities, and creating legacies that inspire generations. To any woman reading this, I say: carve out your own path. Don't wait for permission or the perfect time, because those things rarely come. Start where you are, with what you have, and build from there.

Vera Firman

Vera Firman is a trailblazing entrepreneur with a story that exemplifies resilience, adaptability, and the power of bold ambition. Born and raised in the modest Crimean town of Kerch, Vera's early life was shaped by economic hardships and cultural limitations. Yet, from a young age, she dreamed of breaking free from her environment to create a legacy of her own.

At just 20 years old, Vera moved to Dubai, embracing a new culture and language while pursuing higher education and building her career. In the years following that move, she has co-founded a thriving Dubai consulting firm, launched VF Agency, a leading US SEO agency, and founded Pulse Growth to help businesses scale successfully.

A proud wife and mother, Vera balances her personal life with her professional aspirations, drawing inspiration from her family while empowering others to follow their dreams. She is passionate about inspiring women from all backgrounds to overcome fears, embrace challenges, and lead boldly. Through her journey, Vera embodies the values of courage, discipline, and vision, proving that circumstances don't define potential. She remains dedicated to leaving a legacy of empowerment for future generations of women entrepreneurs.

You can follow Vera on LinkedIn at https://www.linkedin.com/in/verafirman or Instagram at https://www.instagram.com/vera_firman – and if you have any questions, don't be shy to send a DM.

Afterword

Your Chapter Awaits

Dear Reader,

As you turn this final page, you might find yourself reflecting on the journey you've just experienced through these words. Each story you read is a tapestry of dreams, struggles, triumphs, and the relentless spirit of its creator. Now, imagine a world where your story joins these ranks – where your voice, your experiences, and your unique perspective are shared and celebrated.

This is not just an invitation; it's a call to action from the curator of this book, Cathy Derksen, the owner of Inspired Tenacity. Cathy believes in the power of stories to transform, inspire, and connect humankind. More importantly, she believes in your story and its potential to make a significant impact on the planet.

Why wait for "someday" to tell your story? The time is now, and the world is ready to listen. Whether it's a tale of adventure, a deeply personal memoir, a groundbreaking idea, or a story that has been quietly growing in your heart, it deserves to be told.

Inspired Tenacity specializes in turning visions into reality. Cathy understands the journey of transforming a personal narrative into a published book – it's a journey of courage, creativity, and breaking through fears. Cathy and her team are dedicated to guiding you through every step of this exhilarating process, from the initial draft to the moment your book is held in the hands of eager readers across the globe.

Join her vibrant community of authors, a diverse group of storytellers who have dared to make their voices heard. You'll discover a supportive network of mentors, editors, and fellow authors who are all committed to the success of your story.

Take the leap. Embrace the thrill of seeing your own story in a book. Contact Cathy at InspiredTenacity.com, and embark on this remarkable journey together. Your story matters, and the time to share it with the world is now.

p.s. Remember, every great story begins with a simple decision to start writing. Yours is no different. Let's make it happen, together.

READER BONUS!

Dear Reader,

As a thank you for your support, Action Takers Publishing would like to offer you a special reader bonus. Learn how to become an Amazon bestselling author by downloading "How to Become an Amazon Bestseller—Top Strategies Revealed."

You have a story to tell. It's time to tell it.

If you've ever thought about sharing your story and becoming an author, this ebook will give you tips for after you've published. This comprehensive ebook is designed to provide you with the tools and knowledge you need to bring your book to life and turn it into a successful venture.

Ready to become a bestselling author? Download your copy today at https://actiontakerspublishing.com/bestsellertips. As an Action Taker, you know there's no time like the present.

BS Tips

READER BONUS!

Made in the USA
Las Vegas, NV
07 February 2025

17701975R10128